WINGS

— NOT —

STRINGS

PARENTING STRATEGIES
TO LET GO WITH CONFIDENCE

Dennis Trittin & Arlyn Lawrence

LifeSmart

PUBLISHING, LLC

PRAISE FOR
WINGS NOT STRINGS

"If there were such a thing as 'Teen Experts,' I am positive Dennis and Arlyn would own that title. The research, data, and experience they bring to this book are invaluable to adults and teenagers alike. As a mom of five with three already launched, I often hear, 'You already know this journey; you should be an expert by now.' Truth be told, letting go has never been an easy stage for me. This book could not have arrived at a better time. The written tools and steps to guiding both the launching of our teens as well as our role in letting them go have taken me from questioning my own abilities to now being confident that I can release them to soar. A fantastic book and must read for every parent."
—*Trisha Novotny, Founder, 24/7 Moms*

"Dennis Trittin and Arlyn Lawrence have done what they have been doing with audiences for years—with insight, clarity, warmth, humility, grace, and intelligence they have provided tools for families to shape, and then launch, their children into adulthood, equipped to flourish. In page after page, their counsel is practical and accessible. Dennis and Arlyn communicate their wisdom and reflections in an uncommonly incisive and readable style. For our family, now with adult children starting their own families, this book will be one we provide for their nightstands. No doubt it will serve as a vital resource in their parenting toolbox. We all want the best for our children, and for our children's children. *Wings Not Strings* will contribute mightily to that good and important result, not just for their sakes, but for society's as well."
—*Scott McQuilkin, VP for Institutional Advancement, Whitworth University*

"Parenting in today's culture is filled with so many things for us to be fearful about. Our kids' anxiety is at an all-time high. Then there's technology we have to deal with. We do our best to keep our kids safe and it's not easy. We try to ensure our kids make good decisions and are successful, yet where do we step back or get involved? I am constantly confronted with parents who are striving to do everything right, yet who feel like they're failing. They question and doubt themselves and look for concrete answers. *Wings Not Strings* is the roadmap that provides parents with the answers they are seeking."
—*Sheryl Gould, Founder and CEO,* Moms of Tweens and Teens

Wings Not Strings, Dennis and Arlyn's third book, provides not only the perfect analogy for successfully launching young adults, but also thoughtful, practical advice and strategies on how to raise teenagers in today's complicated culture. *Wings Not Strings* empowered me to see where I may be falling into certain parenting traps and then gave me actionable steps to get back on track to successfully launching my five teenagers. This book should be required reading for every parent!"
—*Amy Carney, Author,* **Parent on Purpose**

"As someone who works with high school students preparing for the launch, I feel this is a must-read book. The information Dennis and Arlyn share is invaluable in preparing not only students, but also parents, for life after high school. Their insights will help equip students to be motivated, responsible, and productive citizens ready to face an ever-changing world."
—*Todd Davis, Counselor, Gig Harbor High School*

"While we hear a lot of general complaints about 'this generation,' and murmuring about their problems and attitudes, Dennis and Arlyn have gathered data and found the truth. They truly understand the pressures and challenges families face and share the tools we need to help our kids navigate the teen years in a way that prepares them for a successful transition to adulthood. Their goal of teaching us to parent with a vision of releasing an eagle to soar to the heights, rather than a kite we continue to control—giving children wings, not strings—is a beautiful one. It's also one that relieves the stress of parenting and guides us to doing what's best for both our children and ourselves in the long run, making this book a compassionate, timely, and powerful resource for parents."

—*Sandy Fowler, Co-Founder and Podcast Host, Mighty Parenting*

"If there is one role that will impact the world the most, it is parenting. Our kids need a solid foundation and healthy communication and leadership, because today's kids are tomorrow's hope. *Wings Not Strings* is a practical and insightful guide for any parent, and the tools in it are crucial to raising strong, independent, and empowered kids who turn into exceptional adults. Whether you have young kids or kids about to launch, this book will be immensely helpful."

—*Noel Meador, Executive Director, Stronger Families*

"*Wings Not Strings* is a parenting book for all! Any parent, guardian, grandparent, or adult who cares for the young adult(s) in their life will benefit from reading and applying the suggestions and advice provided in this book. We all want to raise children that are happy, healthy, considerate, caring, and productive members of society. This book will help us all with just that. Thank you, Dennis and Arlyn, for a job well done!"

—*Pam Wickman, Life Skills Teacher, Kimberly High School*

Wings Not Strings: Parenting Strategies to Let Go with Confidence
First Edition Trade Book, 2019

Published by LifeSmart Publishing, LLC. Gig Harbor, WA 98332.

To order additional books:
www.parentingforthelaunch.com
www.dennistrittin.com
www.amazon.com
www.btpubservices.com

ISBN: 978-0-9909603-0-0

E-book also available:

ISBN: 978-0-9909603-1-7 (ePUB)
ISBN: 978-0-9909603-2-4 (ePDF)

Published by LifeSmart Publishing, LLC, Gig Harbor, WA
www.lifesmartpublishing.com
Editorial and Book Packaging: Inspira Literary Solutions, Gig Harbor, WA
Book Design: Samantha Jones
Printed in the USA by Baker and Taylor

Dedicated to all the devoted parents
who are doing their best to position their
children to succeed in the real world.

We honor you!

TABLE OF CONTENTS

INTRODUCTION

"Few transitions bring as much joy, tears, and anxiety to parents as when their children graduate from high school and head off into the 'real world.' It's a strange concoction of emotions that is one part reflection (all the memories), one part conviction (did we do everything we could?), and one part wonder (how will they do?). Questions race through our mind:

'Have we taught them everything they need to know?'
'Are they on the right track?'
'Will they make good decisions?'
'How will our relationship change?'
'Can they live successfully as independent adults?'
'Are they ready?'
'Are we ready???'

As a parent, you play the vital role in preparing your teen for a successful launch. No doubt the past fourteen to seventeen years or so have flown by quickly. Now, you're on the verge of seeing him or her off into the next season of life. If you're like us—and most of the other parents we meet—you want to make sure you've done everything you can to set him or her up for success.

Letting go of a young adult child can be hard—and it always seems to come sooner than you think. When it does happen, as it inevitably will, we want to let them go with confidence and watch them soar to success in every area of their lives.

We (co-authors Dennis Trittin and Arlyn Lawrence) wrote these words back in 2013 when we released our book, *Parenting for the Launch: Raising Teens to Succeed in the Real World*. And, they are as true today as they were six years ago.

Since then, we have had numerous opportunities to speak with parents and parenting experts on the topic of raising and releasing teens into the real world. We've witnessed triumphs and trials both before and after the launch, and it's been an honor to mentor parents navigating their unique situations. We especially enjoy Q&A sessions to hear what's in the hearts and minds of today's parents.

Without a doubt, this one question surfaces in every talk, podcast, or interview: "When, and how, do I let go?" We appreciate the transparency in a question like this. Translated, the "when" usually means, "we're not there yet," and the "how" means, well, "How?!?" Although we addressed this question in *Parenting for the Launch*, we decided to delve deeper in this new book. The fact is, many parents are struggling mightily with letting go, and countless young adults are finding life on their own to be a rude awakening. *Make no mistake, these experiences are linked.*

Why are the adolescent years such a challenging season for parents? There are several reasons, not the least of which is that many are simply unprepared to deal with the pressures and changes in their kids. It happens so quickly and intensely that parents can be caught off guard. Also, with comparatively few support groups for parents of tweens and teens, they can feel alone and disconnected. Finally, let's be honest: when we contemplated having kids, we weren't exactly imagining teenagers—and all that comes with that!

There is another important factor at work. Most parents are so focused on their *kids* that they can underappreciate how significant this transition is for *them*. We need to remember: while high school graduates are closing a chapter on their childhoods, parents are also closing a chapter of their own. So, in order for a launch to be a successful, it means that *both* parents and teens are prepared and confident. Generally speaking, when parents aren't, their kids aren't either.

In our experience, when teens aren't ready to launch, it is often because their parents didn't, figuratively speaking, move over from the driver's seat to the passenger seat in their child's life. The end result is a teen who remains stuck in Neverland—a kind of part-child, part-adult place in life. Unfortunately, this has become a pervasive issue.

The good news is that there is a better way—to parent with a vision of releasing an eagle to soar to the heights, rather than a kite we continue to control. It's giving children *wings, not strings*. It's being strategic and purposeful about parenting a *future adult*.

Wings are the empowering things we do to prepare our children to be secure, confident, and independent adults, who will live with purpose, integrity, and impact. We grow wings when we train them with strong internal guiding principles and give them freedom, opportunity, and accountability to apply those principles responsibly. Like an eagle, they are free to explore far and wide, while navigating the turbulence life often brings.

Strings are anything that ties down our children and prevents them from achieving their full potential. We constrain them when we control and manage them with a tight grip—even as they mature through the teen years.

It can also happen when we pressure, coddle, enable, or ignore them. Regardless of which extreme, they are inhibited rather than equipped and empowered. Picture a kite— it can never fly freely to its natural destination. It is tied down, constrained, and maneuvered by the person controlling the strings. This is the end result **when parents allow nurture to interfere with nature**.

We wrote this book because so many families are struggling with what ought to be a natural evolutionary process. To counter these influences and help you with your family's eventual launch, we tackle these important topics in this book:

> » current perspectives from organizations (e.g., colleges and employers) receiving our graduates and the reasons for these outcomes, including parenting styles
> » empowering parenting strategies that grow wings, not strings
> » when and how to let go (moving from driver to passenger)
> » building the personal leadership skills children need for adulthood
> » strategies for dealing with adolescent anxiety and technology
> » the prize that awaits when parents navigate this successfully

We hope this book encourages and equips you, and that you will take the opportunity to self-evaluate your parenting style and methods as you read through it. No one, including us (!), is a perfect parent, but we can all stand to sharpen our techniques to be the best we can be. It is a privilege to come alongside you in your parenting journey—to help you parent with purpose and let go with confidence! We wish you and your children every success.

CHAPTER ONE

A CONCERNING YOUNG ADLT LANDSCAPE

A CONCERNING YOUNG ADULT LANDSCAPE

"Houston, we have a problem."
—*Apollo 13* film line

Up until recent years, it seemed an inarguable fact of life in America that most children would grow up attending school, graduate with a diploma signifying their accomplishment of certain minimum standards, and go on to either post-secondary education, the military, or the workforce. They would leave their parents' homes, establish independent households of their own, create economic and emotional self-sufficiency for themselves, find a life partner, and likely marry. They would follow lifelong career paths that would provide them with consistent income and a way to contribute to the community and society at large. Obviously, there would be variations within this path, but that was the typical scenario. And, it is likely still the objective that most parents think they are working towards today.

However, something has changed.

These days, many parents of young adults find themselves navigating a bewildering and peculiar landscape of circumstances that includes such new terminology as "adulting," "technology addiction," "safe spaces," "trigger warnings," and "failure to launch." Many of the statistics on the younger generation are perplexing, if not downright alarming: 30% of college students drop out after the first year and only 40% graduate with a four-year degree. A third of all 18- to 34-year olds live with their parents. Most kids over 13 are spending 60% of their waking moments consuming media.[1] And more children, teens, and young adults than ever before are being treated with medication for anxiety and depression.

It is into this landscape that we are launching our next generation. And, while most parents may not necessarily know the details of why the landscape has become so challenging, most intuitively recognize the perplexities and the perils.

The question is: *what can we do about it?* How can we as parents do our part to raise and release into the world mature, responsible, motivated, and productive citizens who will soar in adulthood, and be the contributing members of their families and communities that we want and need them to be?

What Are We Launching into the World?

Let's consider an analogy. If we (collectively as parents of the younger generation) were manufacturers launching a new product into the world, wouldn't we want to get consumer feedback of that product to evaluate how well we're doing with our development and production? Most surely we would! Now, that may sound like an overly businesslike way to describe childrearing, and it is. But, we offer the analogy to make a point: the outcomes from our parenting methods do impact how our young adults fare and are received and perceived when they enter the real world. *Will they be set up for success or failure?*

With this scenario in mind, we think it's important to begin by sharing some "consumer feedback" we and other experts have been receiving in recent years from employers and post-secondary institutions—the primary recipients of today's graduates. Their real-world perspectives are both telling and alarming.

Employers

In our work with *What I Wish I Knew at 18* (our leadership and life skills book and curriculum), we regularly interact with employers who hire students and graduates. As a publisher focused on training the next generation, we value their objective assessments of the workplace readiness of their younger employees.

Without exception, we are hearing an overwhelming and urgent cry. They tell us the current generation of young adults, generally speaking, is emerging into the world and their workplaces grossly unprepared. *To a person, they stress that it wasn't always this way.*

Importantly, we believe these employers' desires and expectations are reasonable. When asked what qualities they are seeking in their employees, they cite practical life skills such as communication, problem solving, high-quality standards, and professionalism, as well as personal leadership skills such as integrity, dependability, work ethic, team-mindedness, resourcefulness, and resilience. As parents, we think we can all agree these are worthy attributes to aspire for in our children.

How is this squaring with the *actual* experience of employers? Importantly, they commend their younger employees for their creativity, innovation, tech savvy, global awareness, and desire to make a positive impact on their community. That's great and worthy of praise. But, in general, employers find them lacking in the desired qualities/skills listed above. Their most common complaints include an entitlement mentality, poor work ethic, unreliability, lacking manners/interpersonal skills, difficulty handling constructive feedback, distraction, and disrespect.

Now, take note: these are not life skills that have generally been taught in schools (although we argue they should be). No, most of these qualities and skills have historically been the primary responsibility of the family to instill. Parents, we need to take this to heart and own it.

Oddly, many parents do recognize the deficiency, but, instead of training to the deficit, they try to compensate for it themselves (enabling) or control their children's environment to manage it (helicoptering)—even when those "children" have become adults. Believe it or not, parental intrusion in the workplace has become a new and deeply frustrating issue for employers. Examples include irate calls by parents to managers on behalf of their children, completing their job applications, and even coming to their job interviews! This is *no* joke. Yes, Houston, we *do* have a problem.

Universities

Higher education institutions are reporting similar issues on their campuses. Our conversations with university presidents, advisors, professors, and counselors, and their high school counterparts, echo many of the employers' concerns. Within their academic settings, they cite student deficiencies in handling pressure and adversity, disrespect for authority, emotional fragility, and general immaturity. Similar to employers, they also report excessive parental involvement/intrusion (e.g., contacting professors about disappointing grades, completing applications, non-stop texting with their children, etc.).

Statistics provide us with additional markers, illustrating the difficulties today's students are experiencing in their college environments:

» As of 2012, the graduation rate of full-time students attending *four*-year colleges was 59% in *six* years[2]; when part-time and transfer students were included, the number fell to 45%.[3]

» Only 78% of freshman students return to their college in the sophomore year.[4]

» 36% of American graduates regret the college major they selected; the figure is 40% for those with bachelor's degrees.[5]

» The demand for counseling center services by university students is skyrocketing, and administrators are struggling to manage it. According to research summarized in the Penn State Center for Collegiate Mental Health 2015 Annual Report, such demand grew some 30-40% for the previous five years versus only 5% for the student population.[6] Anxiety and depression are the two most common reasons students are seeking professional, mental health assistance on campus.

» Conversations with college students and graduates reveal considerable frustration and resentment over their lack of *practical life skills* training.

When considered together, this paints a picture of widespread struggles and inadequate preparation for the demands of college, career, and adult living. The resulting personal and financial tolls are significant and concerning. For parents of future graduates, it's important to understand this reality to help prevent and manage these risks.

Why We're Missing the Mark

"Little children, headache; big children, heartache."
—Italian Proverb

General Influences

You are likely wondering how we arrived at this state of affairs—where the problems we've just mentioned have become the norm rather than the exception. Unfortunately, it's the result of a multitude of factors and contributors, only some of which involve the family and our parenting. Here are several key reasons for the difficulties many young people are facing as they transition into adulthood:

» High schools generally aren't prioritizing next-step training in their course requirements. Many "adult preparation" courses, such as personal finance, life skills, leadership, independent living, and college/career readiness, if offered at all, are generally electives rather than core requirements. Most colleges aren't filling the gap either, presuming their first-year students have acquired these skills before. The void in *practical living* education is pervasive and disconcerting.

» Parents and educators are often erroneously assuming the *other* is covering these important topics;

students are bearing the consequences of this training deficit and finger pointing.

» The "college for all" mentality is hampering students who are either not college ready or would be better served pursuing other avenues to their careers.

» Grade inflation is producing a false sense of academic prowess that college has a way of exposing; this is a major source of anxiety for young adults.

» Colleges and universities are increasingly coddling students instead of building grit and resilience.

» Many teens are lacking valuable job experience due to tighter government regulations of student workers or involvement in other activities.

» Smartphones and screen time are consuming valuable free time, shortening attention spans, increasing distractions, inhibiting personal communication, heightening anxiety, promoting addiction, and reducing motivation.

» Our culture has grown more casual, caustic, entertainment obsessed, and child-centered at a time when experts are extending the age of adolescence to the mid-to-late twenties. Consequently, maturity levels are not what they used to be.

» Growing family dysfunction and fragmentation are adversely affecting socio-emotional health and support systems and preparation for adulthood.

Parenting Influences

In addition to these general influences, parents also have to accept responsibility for their contribution to the young adult landscape. As primary caregivers, we play the lead role. So, let's put our egos aside and be truly honest with ourselves as we consider the impact of our own *parenting strategies and methods.*

Our goal is to give our children wings, not strings.But the fact is, despite the best of intentions, sometimes our own parenting strategies can get in the way of achieving our objectives. Although our children bear the primary responsibility for how their lives turn out (don't you forget it!), parenting influences can be significant.

We can all agree that we want to see our children happy, of admirable character, and successful. But, the different ways parents try to achieve these objectives can be all over the map. For example, when we (these authors) were growing up, authoritarian parenting was typical. Those were the days of, "Because I said so," non-negotiable orders, and self-sufficiency. Teens were expected to leave home after graduation, whether that meant to college, the trades, a job, or the military. The ball was in the graduate's court to sink or swim. Tough love ruled the day.

Times have changed, in part because of the pitfalls associated with extreme versions of this parenting philosophy. However, as it usually happens, the pendulum swings to the opposite extreme. We overcorrect, and new issues and unintended consequences emerge. Such is the case now, with overprotection, coddling, and control permeating the parenting landscape.

This is the generation of highly involved parenting. Today, fathers are inside the delivery room (rather than pacing in an outside hallway or in the hospital at all!). In many cases, moms (or dads) are giving up lucrative careers to take on the full-time job of parenting. And, when they do, they give it every bit as much effort as they did in their careers. Enter the "professional parents" who . . .

» routinely attend *all* sports and dance practices
» make their teens' beds and pick up after them
» bend over backward to keep their children happy and content
» sometimes DO their kids' homework
» plan their lives around the non-stop schedules and resumé-building activities of their children
» place undue pressure on their children to perform
» when talking with other parents, revel in their own children's accomplishments
» advocate for their children at teacher conferences and school board meetings and defend their children's misbehavior with authority figures
» fill out their children's college and employment applications
» make every personal effort to help their kids make the team, land the lead role, earn a 4.0, get the job, win the promotion . . .

So, is it any wonder why Junior struggles with self-confidence, anxiety, entitlement, motivation, decision-making, problem solving, and the overall demands of adulthood when he or she leaves home? Or why employers and universities are characterizing young adults the way they are? And why parents struggle with letting go when Junior is about to enter the real world?

We'll have much more to say about the role of parents in our next chapter when we explore the nature and impact of today's most common parenting styles. Suffice it to say, when it comes to parenting, Houston, we have a problem, too.

TAKE FIVE

1. How does the employer perspective described above square with your own experiences with the younger generation in a work context? Were there any surprises? Based on feedback from both employers and universities, how might their perspectives influence how you prepare your teen for the launch?

2. How did the "parenting influences" list resonate with you? What other factors would you add to the list?

3. Finally, how would you assess the degree to which your children's schooling is *practically* preparing them for independent life? Which topics and subjects do you need to take the lead on to ensure the bases are covered? Don't assume that these are being covered by other parties!

CHAPTER TWO

THE EFFECTS OF PARENTING STYLE

═══════╲╱═══════

"Before I got married I had six theories about bringing up children; now I have six children and no theories."
—John Wilmot

In the last chapter, we briefly highlighted the impact that some of the current childrearing models are having on the well-being and outcomes of today's young adults. We simply cannot overstate the significant role that parenting style is playing. Although parents don't intentionally choose a style per se, their tendencies often have philosophical undertones that matter greatly.

So, with that in mind, let's drill down into three of today's most common parenting styles, which, unintended or otherwise, are creating "strings" in many emerging adults. We'll describe these styles, their root motivations, and the resulting consequences we are observing in children and young adults.

Although parenting isn't about "picking a style" and running with it, we do have some tendencies that stem from our background, experiences, desires, and beliefs. You might recognize some of your own habits here—we all will to some degree—but the goal is becoming more self-aware of how our parenting can affect our children in unexpected ways.

Helicopter Parenting

Most of us have had *that* boss. You know, the one who is always looking over your shoulder, making endless suggestions, asking for status reports on the hour, constantly correcting your work, nagging you when you're not perfect, taking credit for your work, making decisions that are rightfully yours, and micromanaging you to death. That hovering boss who is all about control. The boss who drives you crazy!

You can probably see where we're going with this. Yes, as parents, we can be *that* boss to our teens and adult children! And, frankly, they don't like it any more than we do when we're treated this way. The fact is, when we go overboard in pursuing helicoptering strategies with our children, it stunts their social-emotional growth and skill development, and *it robs them of the joy of learning and doing things themselves.* Meanwhile, it deprives them of learning from their mistakes—arguably the best character and resilience builder of all. Finally, it causes major relationship strains that are difficult to overcome.

Figuratively speaking, helicoptering can be likened to the parent who, when teaching his/her child to ride a bike, never lets go of the handlebars. Sure, the child (now teen) stays upright, but is never free to succeed or fail on his/her own. And, these kids are likely to enter adulthood overconfident, due to a false perception that they can do for themselves what their parents did for them. That's a big problem when reality hits!

Here are some common behaviors and telltale signs of this parenting approach:

» interfering with their child's homework to the point of doing it themselves
» micromanaging chores/household responsibilities to the point of doing it themselves
» texting their kids constantly, even during school hours
» choosing their children's friends
» frantically managing their children's schedules and giving endless reminders
» making decisions that rightfully belong to their teen
» overly protecting and rescuing kids from failure or minor risks; restricting them from meeting different people or pursuing age-appropriate activities due to unreasonable fears
» not allowing children to experience enough of the real world to make informed choices of their own

Why is helicopter parenting so common? Here are some of the root causes:

» our desire to control or manage outcomes (and in extreme cases, to exert power)
» a lack of trust and confidence in our children's abilities and judgment
» fear of failure and of the world
» our own insecurities and desire to feel needed
» perfectionist tendencies (we can do it better/faster)
» a desire to be helpful without fully taking into account the long-term consequences

As with any parenting style, if we take things too far, we can actually stunt our children's development. And, with the growth in helicopter parenting, it is no surprise that we are observing the following unfortunate consequences in many emerging adults:

- » low self-esteem and self-confidence
- » weak decision-making and problem-solving skills
- » poor motivation and work ethic
- » lack of resilience and ability to cope with challenges
- » difficulty handling conflict
- » co-dependency

What might a 25-year-old who has been the subject of helicoptering say to his/her parents, upon reflection? As difficult as this would be to hear, it would probably go something like this:

- » "You didn't trust me."
- » "You didn't believe in me."
- » "You always controlled me."
- » "You didn't let me grow up and have a life."
- » "You deprived me of the joy of doing or achieving things myself."
- » "You didn't respect my need for privacy or give me space."

Clearly, these are tough words, but unfortunately realistic. Helicoptering is a self-confidence destroyer in our children.

Finally, it almost goes without saying that helicoptering places severe strains on the parent-child—and, especially, the parent-adult-child—relationship. The desire for more independence in the teen years, if not respected by the parent, builds tremendous resentment. Since most parent-child relationships will occur after our kids leave the nest, that really hurts!

Performance Parenting

Although we naturally want our children to succeed, some parents take this to such an extreme that they appear to value *performance* more than the *person*. They can view their children's outcomes (especially their accomplishments) as a direct reflection of their parenting and apply intense pressure to perform to unreasonable standards. This style is especially common among professionally and economically successful parents who desire the same (or better) outcomes for their children. Not surprisingly, they often fall prey to the peer pressure from other "successful" parents, and expect their children to supply their bragging rights. We know this description sounds harsh, but it is unfortunately common.

Here are some typical behaviors and strategies of the performance-driven parent:

» perfectionist tendencies; excessive emphasis on minor shortfalls
» unrealistic expectations, regardless of the child's ability, interest, personality, and emotional makeup
» verbal pressure to perform and harsh responses (or ridicule) when the child fails to deliver
» competitive comparisons to siblings or other children

» complaints to teachers/professors when grades are lacking, or to coaches for inadequate play time (these are viewed as blemishes on their child's resumé)

» defending their children's misbehavior to authority figures

» placing pressure on their children to pursue the same colleges or careers as their parents (an unfortunate and unhealthy desire to create a "mini me")

It is truly painful to listen to teens who are on the receiving end of this parenting style. For example, in our speaking engagements with students, one of the most common questions we receive is, "How can I convince my parents to let me live my dream when they want me to live theirs?" These kids feel devalued for *who* they are and consider themselves objects to feed their parents' egos. While not generally the intention of the performance parent, this is often the consequence—and it feels very real to their children.

Here are some root causes and motivators behind performance parenting:

» parental pride and ego taken too far

» excessive and misplaced identity in their children's outcomes, and in their parenting role (to the exclusion of other roles in their lives)

» excessive desire for their children's success

» the philosophy, common in coaching, that pressure maximizes motivation and performance

» the belief that parents can/should control their children's outcomes

» susceptibility to peer pressure from other parents

Predictably, here are some telltale signs of children who are living under the guidance of a performance parent:

» lacking self-worth
» anxiety, depression, or worse
» risk aversion and fear of failure
» narrow interests
» isolation
» inability to cope with underperformance or disappointment
» sibling rivalry
» resentment toward, and distance from, parents

If we were to imagine a message to parents from a 25-year-old who was subjected to performance parenting, it would likely go something like this:

» "You didn't care about me, only how well I did."
» "You expected me to be perfect; I never felt my best was good enough."
» "I was afraid to try new things out of fear I might fail."
» "There was never any room in my life for fun or time to just chill."
» "You didn't let me live my dream; you wanted me to live yours."

Ouch.

While all of us should have high standards for our children, we need to be mindful of the risks when taken to excess. The consequences can be, and often are, devastating.

Permissive (Buddy) Parenting

As parents, we have a natural desire to raise happy children and provide a harmonious home environment. And, why shouldn't we? But, as those of us who have launched children can attest, the teen years can be especially challenging as our kids express their independence and the sparks start to fly. The yesteryears seem like a nostalgic cakewalk when parents receive pushback and their voices seem devalued in favor of peers. So, it's not surprising to long for the years when our children were more compliant and respectful when they needed—and seemed to like—us more. This can creep into our parenting if we're not careful—for example, if our desire for happy kids and a peaceful household become paramount.

In response, many parents are pursuing a child-centric approach to life and inadvertently raising children who think the world revolves around them. At the extreme, these parents *abdicate their authority* and let their children effectively run the show.

Here are some common examples of this lenient parenting style:

- » treating their children as their friends, with an intense desire to feel liked
- » failing to enforce discipline, standards, and consequences; enabling
- » catering to their children's desires; making excessive time allowances for technology and other forms of entertainment
- » tolerating disrespectful behavior
- » doing their children's chores

» living vicariously through their children; glorifying in their successes and agonizing in their defeats
» being unable to move beyond the nurturing stage and treat their teen as a future adult

What are some underlying causes of this parenting approach? Here are several:

» disrespect of one's parental authority
» overly prioritizing their child's happiness and a "peaceful" household
» limited interests other than parenting (placing identity primarily in their role as mother or father)
» feelings of guilt, perhaps due to a divorce or a busy career; overcompensating
» lack of energy, especially in light of demanding careers and multiple-job situations
» overreaction to one's own authoritarian upbringing ("I'll never be like my parents!")
» defeatism and family dysfunction; giving up
» co-dependency

And, here are some telltale signs in children affected by permissive parenting:

» entitlement mentality; viewing the world as all about them
» lacking motivation and work ethic
» deficient leadership and life skills
» disrespect for authority figures and rules
» addiction to pleasure sources
» poor time management and productivity

This is how a 25-year-old who was the subject of this approach might reflect to his/her parents:

» "I never knew what really mattered to you; my friends had boundaries and their parents cared when they messed up."
» "You never seemed to have a life of your own with your own friends."
» "I didn't need a 'Disneyland Dad/Mom.' I needed structure and accountability."
» "I wish you'd pushed me a little more."
» "I was so unprepared when I left home."

Isn't it interesting that many employer complaints described earlier result from this parenting style? This suggests that it is growing more common. When we consider these parenting styles, it's easy to understand how they find their way into our own practices. Of course we want our children to do well and be happy. However, in the teen years when the clock is ticking and we receive more pushback, parents often respond by giving in or controlling to an unhealthy degree. Striking a proper balance is every parent's challenge—one we'll take up in the next chapters.

TAKE FIVE

After reading and reflecting on this chapter, we hope you have a greater appreciation for the nuances of some common parenting styles and how they influence young adult outcomes. We also hope you consider whether any might be evident in your particular situation. Which, if any, of these parenting behaviors are you most prone to practice? Are there any concerning characteristics in your children that might be linked to your parenting methods? Are any midcourse corrections in order? Any "strings" to address?

CHAPTER THREE

THE SOLUTION: EMPOWERING PARENTING

—————≫—————

If you want children to keep their feet on the ground,
put some responsibility on their shoulders."
—Abgail Van Buren

So, how can we turn the tide? How can we as parents position our families for a successful launch and circumvent many of the issues we are observing today? How can we give our children wings, not strings, and move confidently from the driver seat to the passenger seat in their lives?

The Four Big Changes Facing Young Adults

Before getting into the specifics of these questions, let's identify the four major changes our children will experience as they transition out of their parents' care into independence. By keeping these perspectives in mind, we can increase our level of understanding and empathy and communicate more effectively.

When teens reach the launch stage (roughly the year before and a few years after leaving home—usually 17-20), they are embarking on a new life phase that is pivotal to their future. Because they're one part child and one part adult, and their maturity levels are not all the same, how soon and how well they navigate this stage can vary. Some transition into adulthood better than others. It's just a fact of life. But, how well their parents handle it plays a crucial role, too!

Here are some major challanges teens face as they enter adulthood:

1. *They're in the driver's seat now.* Their parents are transitioning into the passenger seat, and their own lives will never be the same. It's a time of mixed emotions for teens because their childhood is fading into the past and they're starting to take charge of an uncertain future. So, we shouldn't be surprised if our children grow more quiet, contemplative, and anxious at this time and want to spend more time with friends. They're processing an incredible amount of change, so their parents need to be understanding, encouraging, patient, and thick-skinned during this stage.

2. *Major life decisions are at hand.* As they move over to the driver's seat, there's very little time before they are faced with key decisions that will set the tone (and path) for the rest of their lives. Decisions regarding post-secondary education/training and career (or service) will position them on their pathway to independence. They'll manage their finances, develop important disciplines, and perhaps meet the love of their dreams. The pressure intensifies because these decisions are far more impactful than those made before. Consequently, they'll need to think more strategically in a world that tells them to live in the moment. This is no easy adjustment.

3. *Life becomes increasingly competitive.* Over the last few decades, we've witnessed the self-esteem movement where everyone gets a prize. Is it any wonder, then, that

so many young adults are having difficulty handling the increasingly competitive landscape in college and the job market? Whether it's not being accepted into their preferred college or not landing their dream job, they'll soon realize that life is a competition and is not always fair. They'll need to build their competitive edge and, perhaps, take an entry-level position just to get their foot in the door. Personal initiative will soon make or break their future success. Most aren't fully prepared for this rude awakening.

4. *Their ability to form new, healthy relationships will be critical.* The social transitions into and out of college (or elsewhere) are arguably among the most significant changes people experience in life. These relocations often result in growing distance from friends and family, and create challenges with making new friends and settling into their new environment. This has huge social implications and places a premium on their ability to cultivate new friendships. Some young adults are better at handling this than others.

These changes are a lot to absorb in a compressed time frame and important to keep in mind, for us and for them.

What Teens Need from Us

Clearly, all of this change portends a significant transition for the entire family (including close siblings). But, because we previously experienced this stage ourselves as teens, parents are in a special position to offer empathy, encouragement, and perspective. To that end, let's remember what our children need from us at this pivotal time:

» *Our unconditional love and understanding.* No, we may not always like each other, but the security of our love is their safest space.

» *Our belief and encouragement.* When they know how much we believe in them and their future, they'll feel the wind at their back.

» *Practical wisdom and training for independent living.* We need to equip them with nuts and bolts skills (changing a tire, balancing a checking account, doing their laundry, etc.) and the personal leadership skills to successfully navigate adulthood.

» *Our perspectives of their uniqueness and value.* By helping them build self-awareness and an understanding of their worth, they'll develop hope, belief, and a positive vision for their lives. Affirming their uniqueness and value is paramount in the teen years when they are changing so much.

» *Full acceptance that it's their life and dreams, not ours.* Enough said.

» *A healthy and enduring relationship based on mutual trust.* This will plant the seeds for a flourishing adult-to-adult relationship in the near future.

» *An open door, 24-7.* Life happens. They will make mistakes and have regrets just like we did and do. When you show that you are *available and approachable* no matter what, they will be more comfortable seeking your counsel and viewing you as an advocate and asset.

» *Realistic expectations, grace, and a long-term view.* They are experiencing enough pressure as it is and will appreciate your grace in letting them find their way, at their pace.

The Empowering Parent

Now, armed with this background perspective, it's time to get strategic! If our goal is to raise well-prepared, self-confident *future adults* ready to fulfill their dreams and purpose, our parenting philosophy and approach need to be aligned accordingly. Otherwise, our outcomes and theirs will be random, at best. This means we need to be purposeful and intentional in our parenting methods and always keep our goals in mind. With busy lives and a laundry list of daily "to dos," this can be challenging!

As teens mature, it's time to say "good bye" to a control-oriented approach and "hello" to one of coaching and empowerment. This means adopting the role of chief encourager and influencer and shifting away from micromanager. Wise parents like you will give your teen the freedom to grow into their own person, make more of their own decisions, take greater responsibility for themselves and their outcomes, and experience different people and situations with trust and grace.

Importantly, however, the incremental freedom and privileges we give should be earned through our children's demonstrations of maturity, responsibility, and integrity. By adopting such an empowered parenting approach, we give our children one of the greatest gifts of all—our belief in them.

So, how do we actually DO empowered parenting? There are several categories of suggestions we recommend you make a part of your parenting approach. These include:

» philosophy
» communication

» training (we'll address this and the following category in Chapters Six and Seven)
» encouragement

Empowering Philosophy

Philosophically, it all starts with adopting an empowering parenting *mindset*. As children age, parenting strategies should be transitioning from control to coach and influencer. We need to fully embrace that we are no longer raising a child, but, rather, a future adult to reach his/her potential. This mind shift makes a world of difference, and helps us move naturally from the driver's seat over to the passenger seat in our teen's life. Here are some suggestions to consider as you embrace this mindset:

1. *Establish strategic parenting goals.* Productive people are goal setters, and this applies equally to our parenting and families. In Chapter Two of *Parenting for the Launch,* we discuss the merits of a family/parenting mission statement, taking a page from the business playbook. The goals and values you'll develop to guide your children and create your family's brand make a great team-building project. Common family goals bring focus, unity, and purpose. (You can learn more by clicking on the "LifeSmart Parenting Mission Statement" option within the Resources tab at www.dennistrittin.com.)

2. *Keep in mind that you're parent, not friend.* When our children are little, there's a maturity *chasm* between us. However, that gap narrows (at often breakneck pace!)

in the teen years, and even more so in the adult years. When this gap shrinks, and concurrently, when our teens exert more independence and pushback, many parents give up their rightful authority position and move into a friend-type role. To keep the peace, they start letting Junior rule the roost, which can lead to chaos and disrespect. It's critical to maintain gentle authority while they're still under our guidance and responsibility.

3. *Remember, it's their life.* This may seem to contradict #2 above, but when held in healthy tension, actually does not. The difference is the driving philosophy that *raising self-confident children is about them, not us.* It's about helping them reach their potential. This requires healthy separation (understanding that teens are their own persons separate from their parents) and incrementally giving them space and respect as is due any person. If we hold on and impose our desires, it will deprive them of the freedom they need to soar and will build resentment. As parents, we need to give ourselves that same freedom—knowing we are not totally and ultimately responsible for the lives of our children.

4. *Teach for independence.* It's no secret that the best way to learn is by doing. And, yet, parents often fall into the trap of doing things for their children that they can and should be able to do themselves (and will definitely need to do on their own!). So, instead of doing it for them, show them how to do it and let them do it. These teachable moments are a vital step in developing the practical life skills they'll need to master as they enter adulthood. You can start by making a list of these skills and developing an informal plan for building them.

Empowering Communication

Good communication is essential to creating and maintaining good relationships. Arguably, this matters more in the adolescent years than in any other stage when our children are changing dramatically and facing new pressures. It requires an investment of quality and quantity time to do this well. "I didn't spend enough time with my children" is an all-too-common regret you never want to carry! Stay fully engaged, and be willing to compromise your own convenience for those precious times your teen wants to talk. Always look for opportunities to enter their world, and, by all means, don't forget to have fun. It's so easy to fall into the trap of taking *everything* seriously in this season.

Here are some helpful tips for communicating well and building an enduring relationship with your emerging adult:

1. *Employ empowering communication strategies.* In *Parenting for the Launch,* we devote an entire chapter to communication tips that work with teens and young adults. Among our top suggestions are: 1) meet them where they are (be mindful of where and when they open up most), 2) time your difficult conversations wisely and keep your cool at all times, 3) focus more on listening than speaking *(think "share with," rather than "talk to"),* and 4) invite them into your decisions and respect their opinions.

2. *Remember that **how** you say something can matter more than **what** you actually say.* Consider tone of voice, choice of words, body language, and facial expression when you communicate, and avoid showing anger, condescension, and sarcasm. This advice works in other areas of your life, but especially so in communication with your

children. We endeavor to put our best foot forward with our friends and co-workers, don't we? It goes a long way when we give our teens the same consideration.

3. *Treat them and talk to them like grownups and leaders.* As you adopt the "raising a future adult" mantra, you'll need to walk the talk through your words, actions, and expectations. Talk to them like they're a leader and in their mid 20s, and share *why* you decided one way or the other (avoid the "because I said so" approach). Give them the big picture of the longer-term consequences of key decisions and choices. Forward and discuss relevant articles and videos about young adult life and contemporary issues.

4. *Resist the temptation to solve their problems and manage their performance.* If there is one thing that robs children of being self-sufficient, independent, and responsible adults, it's when parents persist in providing all the answers and controlling outcomes. Micromanagement is a self-confidence destroyer that hampers decision-making and delays maturity. If they come to you with a question or for advice, ask for their opinion before offering yours. Keep your focus on building independence and problem-solving skills. It's key to building trust.

These are just a few thoughts to help you get started. Think about how you like to be communicated with by others. Have you afforded your teens the same consideration and respect? This is a difficult shift to make, but parents who are able to make it during the high school years gain a tremendous advantage in building an enduring relationship into the adult years.

TAKE FIVE

1. How does the empowering parenting philosophy we've described compare with the way you were raised? What would you like to do differently than your own parents did? Why? What would you like to emulate?

2. Is communication a strong suit or a growth opportunity for you? How about for your family in general? When reading this chapter, did any ideas come to mind for how you can improve communication with your teen?

CHAPTER FOUR

MOVING FROM DRIVER TO PASSENGER

"The most important thing that parents can teach their children is how to get along without them."
—Frank A. Clark

Now, let's turn to one of the greatest challenges for parents and the catalyst for this book: how to emotionally and relationally let go. To be clear, we're not arguing for cutting ties like some critics of the term "letting go" would have you believe. Rather, it's learning how to loosen the reins naturally in order to position our children for independence. It's a fundamental role change we all need to accept and embrace. We're still actively involved, just differently.

Going from director to chief encourager is a pivotal transition for parents during the years leading up to and including the launch. Change isn't easy for most of us, especially when it comes to something as profound as letting go of our most-valued treasures, our children. *The test of your good parenting will be how well they can do all the things you trained them to do—without your reminding them.* And the time to start practicing, if you haven't already, is now. Yes, now.

The Privileges and Responsibilities of Adulthood

Teens are constantly tugging at the reins, wanting more freedom and goodies. So, when yours asks to be treated like an adult, what he or she really wants are the *privileges* of adulthood. A car. Spending money. A smartphone. Decision-making authority. Autonomy. A later curfew. Unfortunately, because of the nature of childhood (immaturity), and the tendency of some parents to rescue, pamper, and enable, that day never comes, or doesn't come soon enough.

The reality is that most teens are ready for more responsibility than we give them, and they need opportunities to exercise it. Adults have extra rights and privileges that kids look forward to enjoying and naturally want now. But, with adults, those privileges are usually attached to responsibilities. If we give them the privileges, but don't require responsibility, we set them up for an entitlement mentality—and for struggles in the real world.

So, the next time your teen tells you he or she wants to be treated like an adult, do it! Treat him or her like a real adult—not just with privileges, though. Make sure there are responsibilities attached and explain the connection. You don't need to give up full control all at once, but you can start by requiring them to do things like:

» contribute to their own income by getting a job (strive to build enough capacity in their schedules for part-time work)
» buy their own car (or make a significant contribution to it) and pay for all or most of their gas
» pay their portion of the mobile phone bill

» do household chores, run errands, help with meals, and make their own appointments (dentist, doctor, hair, etc.). Encourage them, as is appropriate and realistic, to go to the appointment themselves, fill out the paperwork, etc.

» do their own laundry and make their lunches

» clean up the house before and after they entertain friends

It also means doing *less* of the following:

» constantly reminding

» cleaning up after them and doing (what ought to be) their chores

» doing their homework

» filling out their applications

» allowing their schedules to overwhelm yours

If you are a parent who draws a great deal of identity and personal fulfillment from doing things for your children, it can be difficult to change your habits. You may feel like you're being mean. You might think they're not ready for these new responsibilities. You may be unwilling to live with the fact that the tasks may not be done to your standards. But, if you want to set them up well for the launch and equip them to be happy, healthy, functioning, and successful adults, it must happen. Deep down, we all know this.

No one said this would be easy (it's not), but if you are struggling with the transition to the passenger seat, take some time to self-reflect on the underlying reasons. Be as honest with yourself as you can and commit to taking the necessary steps to grow. This is *especially* true if your main reason for remaining in the driver's seat is because of fear of losing your identity or the sense of being "needed." We have more to say on this later.

A Special Note to Moms (That Dads Should Read, Too)

While having a child leave home can produce feelings of loss in both dads and moms, it is generally moms who feel it most, particularly as it often relates to their own role and identity. More often than not (we realize there are exceptions), it is mothers who are the front-line nurturers. Whether they work outside the home or not, they still tend to be the ones who are the primary day-to-day caregivers in the first 18 years. Because of this, they often experience the strongest sense of loss and emotions.

If the child you are launching is your last or only, you may have the double whammy of experiencing the "empty nest." "Empty nest syndrome" is a psychological condition that produces feelings of grief and/or loneliness when one or more children leave home. IF a woman has placed her primary personal identity in her role as a mother, then the finality of her children leaving home can be traumatic.

If you find yourself feeling weepy, regretful, anxious, and perhaps even lonely, it's vital to allow yourself the necessary time to work through the loss and adjust to your new normal. However, if the feelings become overwhelming or obsessive, or if your anxiety starts turning into behaviors that affect your child who is now living away from home for the first time, you may need to take some extra steps to work through your emotions. Confiding in a trusted friend or faith leader is a good first step. If you have a counselor or therapist you trust, he or she might also be a good option for helping to work through these feelings of loss of purpose and identity.

These kinds of feelings are common, especially when a mom has been pouring so much of her own identity into her role as mother. Letting her grown children go and giving them wings can seem like losing her very "self." We see this manifested in so many different ways—coddling, doing too much for them, obsessive texting/calling, and saying things like, "My baby is leaving . . ."

Actually, your *baby* is not leaving. We'd encourage you not to say this in front of your kids or post this on social media for them to see. Your young adult is not your "baby" anymore, and they may interpret these comments as an indication that you don't want them to leave and you still want them depending on you. Truly, we have seen how this can influence their decision where to go next (choosing a local option to keep mom or dad happy) and how well they will do when they get there. At the very least, it can create unnecessary and undeserved guilt when teens leave their home territory. Bottom line, this kind of messaging can be just another form of strings.

We want to encourage you to give your kids freedom to grow—and start enjoying some freedom yourself! If you are struggling with the thought of losing your identity as your child moves into this next (independent) season of life, keep in mind that YOU are much more than your child(ren)'s mom! In fact, here are some things you can do to move forward with excitement and confidence as it relates to your own personal development and a new level of relationship with your adult child.

As it relates to yourself:

- » If you are grieving, acknowledge it; don't stuff it. You don't have to tell everyone how you're feeling, but do tell those closest to you. They can offer encouragement and helpful tips.
- » Find some positives about the new situation and actively take advantage of them. Do you now have an empty bedroom you can redecorate and turn into another kind of useful space like an office, craft or workout room, or guest room? Do you have more time in your schedule that you can use to go back to school or do something you've been itching to do? Is there a career (or career change) in your future, a hobby you've wanted to start, or a volunteer opportunity at a local charity?
- » Treat yourself. Moms often put themselves last in priority. Put yourself first for a change!
- » Build new friendships or renew old ones. The ability to spend more time with friends is a great benefit of your transition from full-time parent to parent-with-kids-launched.
- » Spend some time with yourself! If you've been a busy mom, being "alone" more will be a novelty. *What will I do with myself?* you may wonder. This is a good time to get to know yourself again.
- » Set new goals and dream new dreams, both individually and as a couple, if applicable. You have newfound capacity and freedom to expand your horizons. This is your time, too!

As it relates to your relationship with your adult child:

» Resist the urge to emphasize your loss to your son or daughter. It can cause guilt and come across as being needy and manipulative (even though that's not your intention). Try to communicate in a positive, unemotional, and empowering way, despite your own feelings.

» Schedule regular times for phone calls (decide these in advance) and don't inundate him or her with calls, texts, or Facebook messages. And, don't take it personally if your child fails to reply as frequently or timely as he or she once did. Young adults are experiencing so many new things, and they have a busy schedule with other demands, too.

» Let them make their own plans and decisions without second-guessing them or asking for regular reports (this is more and more applicable the older they get). Most of us in our generation didn't have our parents looking over our shoulders and critiquing our lives the way the current younger generation often experiences. Try to be mindful of this.

A Special Message to Dads (That Moms Should Read, Too)

Okay, guys, now it's your turn.

During our conversations with teens and young adults, we often observe another common theme. At this pivotal time of life where change is constant and key decisions are on the horizon, many kids lack a sense of self and an appreciation of their worth and value. These conversations are painful because kids are searching so hard for something we parents should freely give: unconditional love, our belief in them, and affirmation of their uniqueness and value. For too many, they feel valued for *what they do* more than *who they are*. This obviously hurts and creates self-doubt.

Although fathers are not singlehandedly the culprits by any means, men often struggle expressing their feelings and affirming their kids. They tend to be more direct and task-focused in their communications and erroneously assume, *Our kids know we love them,* even if not expressed. Dads, please don't take this for granted.

Here's a great opportunity to up your fathering game. It is extremely meaningful to our kids and our relationships when we affirm them. Our words, whether spoken or written in a note of expression, are huge sources of self-confidence, support, and encouragement. They need this, and you'll benefit, too. What do you admire most about your kids? Do they know it or are you just assuming they do through osmosis? Whatever way works best for you, just find a way. It's such a gift to your kids.

Simply put, it's one of the most powerful ways to grow wings in our children.

TAKE FIVE

1. How are you preparing yourself emotionally and practically to move over to the passenger seat? Which, if any, factors are holding you back?

2. Are you thinking ahead to your transition, and that of your teen, and how you are going to approach it? How well do you feel your parenting style and practices are preparing your teen to be a successful, independent adult?

3. What are some ways you have been incrementally releasing control and empowering your children to make more of their decisions and assume greater responsibilities? If this is not happening, when and in what areas will you start?

CHAPTER FIVE

BUT WHAT IF I'M *REALLY* STRUGGLING?

―――――✦―――――

"Let your children go if you want to keep them."
—Malcolm S. Forbes

"To let go is to love. I can do both and I can survive."
—Sandy Swenson

A sales manager at a Fortune 100 company shared a baffling recruiting experience with us. He had narrowed his candidate search to three finalists, saving the "best" for the last interview slot. He described his dismay when the 24-year-old man had brought a surprise guest to his final interview—his mother! Yes, his mother.

The manager immediately paused the interview to have a private conversation with the uninvited guest. "Ma'am, why are you here?!?" he asked.

"Because my son is the best candidate, and I want to do everything I can to see that he lands this job," she replied. To my friend's credit, he promptly declared the interview over. He told the woman in no uncertain terms that her interference was inappropriate, and that she'd best serve her son by never doing such a thing again. We can only hope she heeded this warning.

Granted, this "moving over to the passenger seat" business isn't always easy. But, clearly, this mother hadn't budged an inch! This may be an extreme example, but it illustrates the challenge of this season of parenting. How it specifically affects us will be influenced by our parenting philosophy, the preparedness of our kids, the health of our relationships and self-image, and how we handle change. That's why each of our situations is unique.

For some parents, this transition is a monumental challenge. Some hear the clock ticking and fear they are behind schedule. Anxiety naturally builds as they try to play "catch up." Others approach the launch with a deep, impending sense of loss, even pursuing strategies to delay the inevitable. Others find themselves somewhere in between. As authors and parents of adult children, we understand these feelings and hope this chapter provides some additional encouragement and perspective.

In our judgment, there are several underlying reasons that some parents struggle mightily in this season: 1) fear, 2) performance pressure, and 3) identity. Often, these are interrelated.

Tackling Our Fears

First, let's talk a little about fear—the most unpleasant motivator of all. Some of our fears relate to *ourselves*. As parents, we might worry how our relationship with our soon-to-be adult children may change—will they still need or want us? We might fear conflict or reprisals when we discipline our teens. We might have fears or regrets over the job we've done in preparing our children for independence. Perhaps we fear our children will fail or suffer harm without our direct influence or intervention. Or, we might worry about how our lives will change with a newfound void, especially when we face an empty nest. These fears are perfectly natural and important to recognize and acknowledge. If any of these resonate with you, here are some helpful tips to face and overcome them:

» Remember there is no such thing as a perfect parent or perfect children, so give yourself some slack.

» Understand that your relationship with your new adult will be different but can still be great. Keep building your relationship capital, and these investments will pay off in the future. Sure, your children may not need you in the same way, but they will want you in different ways. And, if your relationship isn't where you would like it to be, remember this is a long-term proposition and it can improve. In many cases, the parent/adult child relationship is much stronger than during the turbulent teen years, so keep a positive and optimistic outlook.

» Recognize that "the school of hard knocks" is historically one of the best educations any of us can receive. Preventing your child from receiving this valuable schooling by refusing to let go can often do more harm than good.

» Know that, no matter how well you've prepared your children, it's up to them to live their lives and make their own decisions. Some of their choices will pan out and others not, *just as it was when we were that age*. We encourage you to read *What I Wish I Knew at 18* together with your teen to help cover the bases of preparation for the "launch" and to build your confidence. This investment of time can help you more confidently move over to the passenger seat and strengthen your relationship.

» Refer to the "Parenting Checklist" in the Appendix of this book to help you evaluate your progress and identify any areas for focus.

» Instead of viewing this change in your household as a loss or vacuum, consider it an opportunity for your own growth. You've sacrificed much during this season of life, and it's your time now. What interests and passions could you pursue that you've placed on the back burner?

Other fears relate to our *children*. For example, will they make good decisions and stay true to the values we taught? Will they be happy and do well? Will they surround themselves with positive people and build healthy relationships? Will they find a well-matched career and succeed? How will they handle the changing culture around them, with which we may or may not agree? To these worries, we offer the following thoughts:

» Depending on their grounding, decision-making, and relationship-building abilities, your adult children may or may not make decisions you would support. But, again, it's their life and you cannot and should not carry the burden of their success or happiness on your shoulders. That's not fair or healthy for anyone.

» The better prepared they are with leadership, life skills, and core values, the more confident they will be AND the more confident you will be. As they mature and demonstrate these skills, it will be much easier for you to envision your eagle soaring, rather than a kite you'll still need to control. Sections of this book, and *What I Wish I Knew at 18*, will guide you in building these skills.

» Remember, success doesn't usually happen overnight and in a straight line. For some children, especially those who are more mature, focused, motivated, and responsible, their path will probably be smoother. Others are late bloomers who may take more time to settle on their direction. Their lives may be characterized by trial and error for several years. By understanding your children and adopting a coaching mentality, you can be a huge asset to them as they find their way.

» Keep your lines of communication open and emphasize approachability and listening in this season. Your teen will increasingly be exposed to new peer pressures and worldviews, so you'll want to create a comfortable environment to discuss these topics. While you may not always agree, your willingness to listen and share is an important show of respect. That's powerful.

» Always remember to affirm them when they demonstrate the core values you and your family hold dear. So often, our compliments relate to accomplishments, rather than to their character. Be sure to value the "who," too.

» Related, encourage your kids to surround themselves with positive peer influences. It is said that you become the average of the five people with whom you spend the most time, so being selective in friend-making is critical.

» Share relevant articles/videos on adulting with them and, by all means, introduce them to other caring adults who can be a part of your informal parenting team. Sometimes, your words spoken by someone else have a better way of sticking!

» Chances are, if you have a forged a strong relationship with your teen, it will endure in their adult years. Young adults have a way of appreciating their parents in ways they may not express in the teen and very early adult years. (You might just have to trust us on this!)

Performance and Identity Pressures

Another common reason parents struggle to let go is that they are placing undue pressure on themselves, and especially on their children, to perform, as if they, the parents, are responsible for their children's success or happiness, when this is not the case. Of course, parents have influence, but our children's eventual life outcomes will largely be of their doing and choices and, appropriately, outside of our control. If this particular pressure is your battle, please release yourself.

Another challenge can be the *parent-to-parent peer pressure* that only exacerbates pressure and anxiety. Not long ago, I (Arlyn) overheard several moms talking about the college visits they were planning or had already completed with their high school seniors. I felt the competition level rise in the room as names were dropped of prestigious schools visited and anticipated. I walked away feeling sorry for everyone involved—parents and children—as the objective was clearly more social posturing and ladder-climbing than it was finding the best fit for their children. Again, if you are feeling this pressure, we encourage you to release yourself.

At its core, if we're honest, performance pressure is a pride and control issue. Shouldn't our children's best be good enough for us? If not, then this is a good time for re-examination and self-correction. Otherwise we risk building resentment and hopelessness in our children, and ourselves.

Misplaced identity is another related issue that can manifest itself in this arena. As mentioned earlier, many parents are so focused on their performance or significance in their roles as mom or dad that it can become the dominant aspect of their identity. This is both unhealthy and unfair for everyone.

Because this one is such a common issue, we encourage you to do some (very honest) self-reflection on this topic. How are you doing on the identity front? Here are some revealing questions for you to consider:

1. How much of your daily thoughts revolve around your children, as opposed to other aspects of your life?
2. How much of your daily life revolves around your children's needs and schedules?
3. What activities and hobbies do you participate in purely for yourself, outside of your children's interests and pursuits?
4. How dependent is your daily disposition on your children's behavior, mood, and performance?
5. To what extent do your children's successes and failures become your "own" successes and failures?

Of course, our role as parent is extremely important, but a healthy balance is necessary, too. **What is particularly worrisome is when parents are driven by their need to feel needed or liked.** In these situations, parents continue to serve and "do" for their children long past the season when it is appropriate, or to an extent that goes above and beyond what is actually necessary. While this serves to reinforce the parent's need for affirmation and significance, it is extremely detrimental for a developing a young adult. Unfortunately, these can turn into unhealthy co-dependent relationships, with the children being the primary victims.

Trying to Make Our Children "Happy"

As mentioned earlier, another common risk to parental success and letting go is when we focus on our children's present happiness as our primary goal. Granted, what parents don't want their kids to like them? However, young children need to learn that what they "ought" to do is not always what they may "want" to do. This is a vitally important lesson at an early age.

Unfortunately, many parents are unwilling to live with the relational tension this reality causes as their children grow. They may fear losing their children's love or friendship. They may abhor conflict, even when it's constructive. Perhaps, in trying to keep their children "happy," they are trying to make up for time spent at the office, or for distance due to travel or divorce. There are numerous reasons why parents can tend toward this extreme. The results of this tendency may not show up until the pre-teen or teen years, and by then it can be difficult to reverse.

Here's an example of how this can start subtly in the early years. Say your toddler is hungry. You ask him, "Do you want a banana or some veggies?" But he wants a bag of chips instead of a banana or veggies. You tell him he needs to eat what is offered to him, and he pitches a fit. What do you do next? You send your spouse/partner out to the store to buy his favorite Doritos! Mom and Dad are happy because Junior is happy. Everybody's happy, right? *Wrong.*

If this style of parenting continues throughout a child's life, as it does for many, what do you think he will grow up thinking? Likely he will come to believe:

» He will always have choices.
» His happiness and satisfaction should be priorities to the people around him.
» He doesn't have to comply with what he is told to do; he rules the roost.
» Mom and Dad will always advocate for him to get his way and come out on top.
» Other people are there to serve him, not the other way around.

Are you seeing these attitudes in your teens, which can result from a lifetime of being made "happy"? If so, you may need to reverse a trend that started a long, long time ago. We're here to tell you: it's never too late.

This scenario may be overly simplistic, but here's the point we want to make: **Out of our desire to provide the best for our children (and keep them happy), some of our parenting methods may be contributing to their perception that the world revolves around them.** If this is the case, they're in for a rude awakening when they leave home and find that the world owes them nothing. And this is exactly what is happening in our culture today—in astronomical proportions. It's called "entitlement." And many times, if we're not careful, our own parenting style can be a root cause of it.

Moving Forward

We encourage you to reflect on the previous sections to see if any of these fears and tendencies may be present in your parenting. If so, try to consider the root causes and address them through your support system or counseling. Fear—no matter how it is manifested—is a powerful force we all need to be aware of and manage.

Admittedly, parenting isn't easy, and we can feel guilt and regret for any number of reasons. Some of the topics addressed here may bring to the surface some issues that might be challenging to face. That's okay! We've all been there. With that in mind, we encourage you to take some quality time for reflection and strategizing. If you are married, and can include your spouse in the process, all the better.

Some action steps might be challenging, especially if they will involve difficult conversations with your children. Don't be surprised if they resist some of your new strategies, especially when their freedoms or privileges are involved. But, by staying positive, treating your children as leaders, sharing the "why," listening well, and if necessary, apologizing and asking for forgiveness, you can create an atmosphere for success.

Finally, please don't be burdened by regrets. Like our children, we are all works in progress, too. A powerful phrase to remember is: "FROM NOW ON." Keeping this in mind can encourage you to accept your imperfections with grace and move forward, a little bit better than yesterday.

TAKE FIVE

1. Are any of the fears we've identified currently interfering with your ability to let go (i.e., to "move from driver to passenger")? Which ones?

2. As a mom or dad reading our personal messages to you, did any of our thoughts particularly resonate—if so, how?

3. Which parenting strategies mentioned in this book do you feel stronger in? Which ones offer your greatest opportunities for growth? Which action steps will you commit to pursue today and in the near future?

CHAPTER SIX

PREPARING YOUR CHILD FOR ADULTHOOD

———— ❥ ————

*"We have to prepare the child for the path,
not the path for the child."*
—Tim Elmore

Adopting an empowering parenting philosophy and embracing the move to the passenger seat will go a long way in preventing the young adult descriptors we discussed earlier. (And, if you only skimmed Chapter One, we encourage you to read it again.)

Given the concerns of employers, post-secondary educators, and students themselves, we believe parents can play a pivotal role in reversing the course and providing the training and encouragement needed to equip their children for success. For example, parents can work to promote a strong work ethic in their children (chores are key), and instill other-centeredness in them (e.g., volunteering to assist the less fortunate). They can teach their kids to seek and accept constructive feedback, develop resourcefulness and self-discipline, learn to problem solve and handle disappointments and conflict, and communicate professionally with adults. These assets and skills build self-confidence and will help them stand out from the crowd.

But, there's more. **The better prepared our children are with wings, the more confident we will be as parents**

in moving over to the passenger seat! When our children demonstrate the personal leadership and life skills and core values needed for the adult world, we naturally feel more comfortable letting go and giving them greater responsibility. This enables the transition from raising a child to raising a future adult. Along the way, it builds trust and mutual respect—so integral to an enduring relationship. The bottom line is this: great preparation is a win-win for all parties.

Avoiding the Derailers

One way we can prepare teens for success after the launch from home is to prepare them in advance to avoid the most common pitfalls that can derail them. The first three months (and year, really) after a teen graduates from high school and leaves home are vitally important, often setting the tone for the rest of a person's college, career, and even life experience. We've all heard the disappointing, if not downright tragic, stories of college careers that ended prematurely due to poor life choices and teens mishandling their new freedom. With that in mind, here are some critical topics related to this transition period that you can begin preparing for *now*—and some prevention measures to discuss *before launch time:*

> » *The social adjustment.* The loss of their convenient support structure, soon geographically scattered, can be hard to take, especially for teens reserved by nature. Often, this leads to intense loneliness and getting into the wrong crowd for the sake of making new "friends" quickly. Social impatience and

insecurity are huge issues for many young adults in new environments as they adjust to being a small fish in a big pond.

Talk about this in advance, so they won't be surprised by feelings of isolation or loneliness. Help them plan some strategies, like meeting everyone in their dormitory floor/workplace department, exploring activity and affinity clubs, working out at the recreation center, studying in the library or student union building, initiating conversations with other students in their classes, and finding people in their major with whom they can study. All of these strategies help make a big place feel smaller. And, emphasize quality over quantity when making new friends by focusing on prospects who share their interests and values.

» *The importance of focus and self-discipline.* Time management, new responsibilities, variable class schedules, endless activities, new roommates, a new job, and the like will be their new reality. Plus, in today's technology-laden world, their devices are enticing, nonstop sources of distraction. The temptation to be playing video games (or surfing Instagram) instead of doing homework can be huge.

This includes financial self-discipline, as well. Far too many students spend their way out of their college experience. Whether they are in college or out in the workforce or military, you can help your teens learn to set up a list of expenses and create at least a rudimentary budget. Encourage them to set aside spending money for the things they want to buy, so they're not tempted to rely on credit cards.

Help them develop a list of priorities and to become master schedulers/planners/budgeters. What's important to them? Grades? Fitness? New friends? Spiritual life? Encourage them to develop daily, prioritized to do lists—and, to eat, sleep, and exercise well. Simply put, life is about time and choices, and discipline will help them make the most out of theirs.

» *Handling academic pressure.* For those attending college, the competition is stiffer, exams and high grades are fewer (putting more pressure on each test), professors are less inclined to offer extra credit, and it's expensive! As if these pressures aren't enough, many parents place unreasonable academic demands to sustain or improve upon his or her high school performance. Remember, it can take students a full year to adapt, especially when they take too many credits or tough courses in the first semester while adjusting to their new reality.

Encourage them to buy and use an academic planner (or app on their phone) that puts all of their exam and assignment due dates, and any extra credit assignments, in ONE PLACE. This way your student can keep track of deadlines and not feel rushed at the last minute when something is due tomorrow. (*What I Wish I Knew at 18* devotes an entire chapter to college academics that might prove helpful to your teen.)

» *Coping with stress.* With their new responsibilities, endless opportunities, and unfamiliar environment, many students experience meaningful and unexpected stressors and adversity shortly after the launch. The college or first time career brings new pressures and outcomes that can be very disappointing, and many are unprepared to deal with it. Yesterday's easygoing kid can quickly become tomorrow's worrywart when experiencing all of this change and challenge.

They need to know they're not alone, they can always reach out by phone, and you will always welcome them when they need a hug or word of encouragement. This is NOT the time to talk about their grades, their student loans, or are-they-looking-for-a-job. This IS the time to speak words of affirmation, encouragement, faith, and hope with sound coaching advice as desired.

It is also a time to discuss healthy stress relievers that work best for them. Examples are a good night's sleep, exercise (especially cardio), a walk with nature, prayer or meditation, music, movies, or coffee with a friend. Understanding their stressors and the best ways to prevent and cope with them is a life skill that pays dividends forever. We tackle this more extensively a little later.

» *Avoiding addictions.* Needless to say, our young adults are exposed to much more when they're out on their own. For a host of reasons, they can easily become addicted to false comforts like alcohol and substances, engage in unhealthy sexual behavior, and become preoccupied with screen time and video games. Clearly, not every student views academics as their top priority! You'll want to have some straight talk with your children so they enter college (or their next step) with their eyes wide open—and with the reality of the consequences of these high-risk choices.

Empowering Training

You may be thinking, *Wow, that's a lot to remember to teach them!* Yes and no. Much of this can be addressed in the context of everyday life. It doesn't necessarily mean you have to sit down and talk about all these topics specifically.

In our experience, it can often be the conversations you have in the car on the way to soccer practice, around the dinner table, or on the beach or hiking trail on a family vacation that provide opportunities for heartfelt discussion and training. Other times, you might want to arrange a scheduled (but relational) time with your teen to talk about some of these topics, like over coffee at a local coffee shop, on a run, or while getting a manicure or pedicure together. For practical topics, it can be when the need for those skills actually arises in your household (e.g., laundry, cooking, car maintenance, etc.).

When that occurs, here are some thoughts for what that "training" for adulthood might include:

1. *Emphasize character over performance.* Success in career and life requires a solid leadership foundation made up of qualities like integrity, reliability, high standards, kindness, respect, other-centeredness, work ethic, humility, positivity, self-control, and manners. These are sustainable leadership qualities that will serve your

children throughout life, as are core values. We encourage your family to review (and self-evaluate with) the "Positive Traits and Values" list in the Resources tab on www.dennistrittin.com. Which are they modeling well? Where could your kids improve and what would help make that happen?

2. *Teach them basic, practical skills for everyday living.* Unfortunately, in most schools, many life skills-oriented courses have gone by the wayside in favor of other options that are nowhere near as relevant. So, it pays to ask your children which particular life skills their school is covering. Examples you may need to lead on are: personal finance (budgeting, banking, credit/debt, spending, identity theft, etc.), cooking, laundry, buying groceries/basics, changing a tire, self-defense, making appointments, choosing a career match, resumé writing, interviewing, and completing college and scholarship applications. Be sure to fill any gaps with your training.

3. *Help them develop strong decision-making skills.* As parents, we need to strategically train our kids to handle real world responsibilities and situations. But, especially for busy, Type-A personalities (or those prone to coddling), this one can be a challenge. If we're not careful, it's easy to for parents to make (what ought to be) their kids' decisions without considering every opportunity as a learning experience. Chances are, we can do it quicker and better, but that's taking the short-term view.

Instead, put your children in situations where they need to analyze options and make decisions (the college/career search is a great example), rather than initiating your solutions. If your teen comes to you with questions like, "How should I handle . . . ?" thank them for asking but have them share their leanings first. This helps build their skills and self-confidence, and you can still offer your advice later. Our book, *What I Wish I Knew at 18*, has a powerful section on mastering decision-making, so you might look into that, too. Finally, by all means, include your children in your family decisions whenever possible. It shows your respect for them and their leadership capabilities, and that's huge.

4. *Cultivate these other important skills.* We encourage you to read the Parenting Checklist in the Appendix of this book for other key preparation topics and skills to build. Among the most important and timely are social skills, personal productivity and time management, self-awareness, handling adversity, and coping with stress. Several of these topics are explored in other sections of this book, and we encourage you to review our book for teens, *What I Wish I Knew at 18*, too.

Empowering Encouragement

In many ways, the teen years are like the perfect storm. Their brains and bodies are undergoing tremendous change. Their social lives—and relentless peer pressure—can be powerful sources of chaos and anxiety. Their academic performance and resumé building can significantly affect their future opportunities. And, they face considerable uncertainty in making their next-step decisions. Is it any wonder why these years are so emotionally and relationally volatile? And why the "terrible twos" can seem like a cakewalk by comparison?

With all this change occurring in a short time frame, it's essential that we approach these years with empathy and encouragement. No, it's not always easy to do, and they may not always show their appreciation, but it is a winning strategy all the same. One of the most important things we can do is to remember we were a teen once ourselves and messed up more times than we can count. This will help us maintain perspective (and our cool!) when it's their turn.

Here are some other strategies that can help you provide the encouragement your teens so desperately need:

1. *Help build their self-awareness.* In the teen and young adult years when children are plotting their future course, it's so important that they truly understand themselves. That means knowing their unique assets, personality, interests, and passions, as well as any constraints holding them back. Self-awareness instills vision, belief, hope, and a sense of value at this critical time. One way to build this quality is for them to create a Personal Balance Sheet. We've developed this valuable tool, which you can find under the Resources tab at www.dennistrittin.com under "Mining the Treasure in You (Personal Balance Sheet)." It will boost their self-confidence, help them understand and appreciate their uniqueness, and bring clarity and vision to their upcoming life decisions.

2. *Surround them with positive influences and adult role models and mentors.* Parenting is a team sport, so use every opportunity to introduce your teens to the great adults in your life! These invaluable third party voices offer friendship, wisdom, encouragement, and connections to help grow their network. (They can also reinforce some key parenting points you've been trying to

get across!) This strategy also builds their communication skills and respect for adults.

3. *Encourage them to stretch themselves and take risks, even if they may not succeed.* In an increasingly competitive, innovative, and interconnected world, it's essential to instill curiosity, initiative, and a "Go for it!" attitude in our children. Help them embrace new experiences and challenges even if the outcomes are uncertain.

   Meeting new people, learning a new skill, leading a project team, applying for a "stretch" job, asking someone out for a date, taking that hard class, and trying out for the team are all part of the journey and build character and resilience. They make our kids more interesting, too! Sure, they won't always win, but giving them the freedom to try and, sometimes, fail, is a gift.

4. *Don't rescue them too quickly.* Of course, if our children are ever in any real danger or distress, we will want to offer assistance. Our teens and young adults should always feel safe and comfortable coming to us for help if they get in a difficult spot. Our goal should be to provide a balance of freedom to fail and support when they do. However, under normal circumstances, we don't want to swoop in too quickly or thoroughly.

   Sometimes falling flat on their faces is exactly what they need—especially to face the consequences of poor decisions. *The children of rescuing and enabling parents have trouble making sound decisions as adults because they don't correlate their actions with consequences.* (Parents who bail out/defend their misbehaving kids at school immediately come to mind.) It also contributes to the entitlement mentality we are seeing all too often.

5. *Consider these memorable launch-time strategies.* The months leading up to graduation and launch time can be chaotic. There are so many activities and to-do items that we often miss out on opportunities to create lasting memories. To combat this, here are two ideas you might want to consider:

A blessing or affirmation packet. Recruit other important people in the lives of your graduate (e.g., friends, relatives, teachers, coaches, mentors) to write letters of encouragement, inspiration, hope, and love. These letters are individually sealed and mailed to the parent who places them in a gift-wrapped box. Of course, parents have to write their own. (Heads up: it may be one of the most emotional things you've ever done!) Then, at an appropriate time, give the gift box of letters to your son or daughter. This will be one of the most meaningful gifts they'll ever receive.

Read *What I Wish I Knew at 18: Life Lessons for the Road Ahead* together. This, our first book, is designed to inspire and equip students for their launch into adulthood. Our 109 life success pointers are conversationally written in a life-coaching style and prepare teens for college, career, marriage/family, and finances. In addition to having a third party voice of wisdom on your side, the book is a powerful parent-teen relationship builder. We invite you to check it out.

TAKE FIVE

After reviewing these strategies, how would you rate yourself as an empowering parent? Rank yourself on a scale of 1 to 10 in the four categories of empowered parenting that we mentioned: Philosophy, Communication, Training, and Encouragement. Where are you excelling? Doing "okay?" Needing improvement? What action steps can you take now?

CHAPTER SEVEN

SHARPENING THEIR PERSONAL LEADERSHIP SKILLS

---❯❯---

"Character is higher than intellect."
—Ralph Waldo Emerson

One of our most important responsibilities as a parent is to equip our children with the personal leadership skills they'll need to flourish in the adult world. These skills, which span our character, ethics, attitude, and relationships, are vitally important, yet often underestimated. To be sure, if this training is inadequate, we will all feel the repercussions when our kids are out on their own.

Unfortunately, one of the greatest myths young people tend to believe is that success is mainly about smarts. Apparently, it was an issue in Emerson's day, too! While intelligence certainly is an asset in life, it is by no means a lock. Ask any employer of young people, and you'll hear this loud and clear: raw intelligence will not make up for a lack of personal leadership and character skills.

One of the best ways to give our children wings (and for us to confidently move over to the passenger seat) is by preparing them for the adult world they will soon enter. For a variety of reasons, many young people are having difficulty relating to adults and fulfilling the responsibilities of the workplace. In many cases, this can be traced to a lack of personal leadership skills development. As advocates for our next generation and those employing them, we thought it worthwhile to delve more deeply into this important topic.

What are employers looking for? In a nutshell, three things:

1. someone who does good (preferably great) work on the job specs,
2. someone who works well with others and, ideally, doesn't require intense supervision, and
3. someone who contributes to the success of the organization and represents its core values well.

We believe these are entirely reasonable expectations. With that, let's explore the personal leadership skills employers are seeking that parents should want their children to model. Based on our own experience, as well as various employer surveys, here is our top ten list of "MVP" qualities to build:

1. *Integrity:* can they be trusted?
2. *Commitment to Excellence:* do they have high standards?
3. *Dependability:* can they be counted on to meet their objectives?
4. *Work ethic/motivation:* do they work hard and are they a self-starter?
5. *Resourcefulness:* are they a creative and efficient worker and decision-maker?
6. *Positive Attitude:* are they a constructive influence?
7. *Team-minded:* do they work well with others and put the team first?

8. *Friendliness:* do they demonstrate kindness and respect to others regardless of the circumstances?
9. *Resilience:* do they handle adversity and solve problems constructively?
10. *Professionalism:* do they demonstrate appropriate manners and communication skills?

Note how these habits will serve your children well in every aspect of their lives, not just in the workplace. Do they tell the truth? How well (and responsibly) do they do their chores? Are they working hard and doing their best in school? How well do they solve problems relating to themselves and others? Are they a good friend? Do they persevere through adversity? Are they respectful to others? Do they display good manners and hygiene? Clearly, there are all sorts of ways you can build these personal leadership skills at home!

Here are a few other training tips:

1. Most importantly, model them yourself.
2. Call out these qualities in your children and in others when they are demonstrated.
3. Seek out opportunities (and some gentle guidance if needed) for them to develop these skills, and honor their efforts when they do.

On a final note, if you have a child who is average or perhaps below average academically, these are wonderful qualities to acknowledge and affirm when their strengths may not lie in "book smarts."

A Closer Look at Work Ethic/Motivation

*"Some people dream of success while others wake up
and work hard at it."*
—Winston Churchill

"The harder I work, the luckier I get."
—Samuel Goldwyn

Based on employer feedback and our observations of today's adolescents, we'd now like to elaborate on two personal leadership skills that seem especially lacking today: work ethic/motivation and professionalism. Here's a true story to set the stage.

Emily (not her real name) landed a part-time job as a server at a local restaurant to help fund her college education. All had gone well as she finished her last semester. Then, one warm summer day, she called in "sick" five minutes before her 5:00 p.m. start time. Clearly, the owner of this family restaurant was angry, inconvenienced, and stunned—especially 20 minutes later when Emily was found posting festive pictures at a beach party some ten miles away. Needless to say, she received her walking papers the next day after arriving on time with a spring in her step.

If you think stories like these are rare, think again. In our conversations with employers of young people, we hear more complaints about work ethic and dependability than about any other traits. Among the examples they cite are: absenteeism, late arrivals, distractions, failure to meet deadlines, deficient work, whining (especially toward more "menial" tasks and perceived injustices), and entitlement attitudes. Consequently, some employers have given up and are now recruiting away from younger candidates.

To a person, they'll tell you it wasn't always this way. And, well-experienced teachers and counselors are citing these same issues in a school context. Countless parents who attend our workshops tell us that their kids (especially boys) lack motivation. It's everywhere, and it's not good.

We believe the responsibility for this generational shift lies primarily with parents. We do our children's chores, either to keep them happy or because we can do them better or quicker. We overcommit them with one activity after another and feel guilty if we also ask them to sweep the garage or clean their room. We allow play to come before work. We permit them hours and hours of time with their endless technology, media, and entertainment options. We do things for them that they can and should be doing themselves. Is it any wonder that attitudes of entitlement and disrespect are so pervasive?

There are many reasons why a strong work ethic and motivation (inextricably linked) are so important in the workplace and in life:

- » They are admired character traits and a MUST for living a productive life and fulfilling our potential.
- » They directly affect our job (and academic) performance, pay potential, reputation, job security, and promotability.
- » Our team members and employers are depending on us.
- » They are key to grit and resilience.
- » They are telltale signs of maturity and responsibility.
- » A strong work ethic can overcome an average skillset.

Here are some telltale signs of people with these valuable attributes:

- » They are self-starters and don't need constant reminders.
- » They don't require rewards each time for hard work; it's intrinsic.
- » They are proactive and take initiative.
- » They are productive and efficient with their time; they focus just as much on working smart as working hard.
- » They are conscientious, take directions, follow policies and guidelines, and are lifelong learners.
- » They avoid complaining about the less interesting aspects of their job/chores
- » They meet or exceed the requirements of the job.
- » They give their employer a high return on investment.

How are you teens faring? Parents, here are some tips for building these essential qualities in your kids:

- » Model them yourselves and teach your children why they are so important.
- » Keep your expectations high; help them envision the leader within.
- » Require age-appropriate chores and hold them accountable (this is where your tough love really pays off!). Introduce them to a wide range of chores, but be somewhat flexible when choosing which ones they are routinely responsible for. Also, give them some chores as a learning experience, especially to develop life skills they'll use on their own (e.g., laundry).

» Limit the amount of time they spend on technology and social media and employ a "work before play" strategy. Too many young people are addicted to entertainment and devices, and it is impacting their motivation.

» Encourage them to be active and curious. If they are struggling with motivation in school, it may be that they're bored. Encourage them to explore other interests and see what surfaces. But, at all costs, do not tolerate laziness.

» Encourage them to choose friends who take these qualities seriously. Peer influences are huge. If our kids surround themselves with positive and productive people, it will rub off. And if they don't, that will rub off, too!

A Closer Look at Professionalism

"A man's manners are a mirror in which
he shows his portrait."
—Johann Wolfgang von Goethe

For young adults who are just entering the workforce, it can be an eye-opening, rude-awakening experience. The demands of the workplace catch them off guard if they are not prepared ahead of time. For example, because our culture has grown more casual (and often coarse) by the year, many employers are now resorting to basic retraining programs. Accordingly, they are emphasizing *professionalism* as an important leadership skill in their employees. *Parents, this presents an opportunity for your teen to really stand out from the crowd and soar!*

When we hear the word, "professionalism," the first thing that usually comes to mind is appearance and language. However, its scope is much broader. So, let's review some of the key aspects of professionalism in a workplace context, but that also apply generally.

Appearance: this includes dress, hygiene, countenance, body language, neatness, cleanliness, posture, etc. Each is important in everyday life, but the bar is that much higher in a professional context. When your young adult starts a new job, encourage him/her to err on the side of more conservative dress and to closely observe how others, especially the most admired employees, appear. They're the best role models to emulate. (Note: This doesn't only apply to a professional "business" setting. No matter what a person's role is on the job—barista, cashier, construction worker, electrician, hair stylist, accountant, teacher, or anything else—they will benefit from maintaining a high standard for their personal appearance.) The impression you make counts for a lot!

Attitude: employers will expect them to arrive on time with a positive attitude and ready to work no matter what. They must try their best regardless of what else is going on in life and learn to compartmentalize their personal life from their professional life. Positivity is a sure sign of a winner!

Excellent Performance: true workplace (and life!) superstars deliver strong performance and contribute to the success of the organization where possible. They go above and beyond with resourcefulness and initiative. They can be relied upon to achieve their goals and meet deadlines. (Obviously, in the teen and young adult years, this equally applies in academic and other settings.)

Manners and Etiquette: these reflect on one's personal standards and respect for others. They are especially important in business/social settings and meetings with recruiters and clients. Your young adult needn't be an Emily Post, but he/she must "show well" to others in basic etiquette. This is a mind shift for many of today's more casual teens.

Ethics and Confidentiality: every employer has basic policies and procedures that must be followed, in addition to laws and regulations. And, depending on the position, employees are often privy to confidential information. Here, your young adult's standards must be *impeccable* and nothing less. A broken trust, or failure to uphold ethics and policies, can be disastrous. Outside of the workplace, this applies in our relationships when people share information in confidence. We may not always be liked or loved, but we must always be trusted!

Representation of Brand: most companies have a mission, vision, and values statement that employees are expected to honor internally and externally. This includes our comments and posts in the public square, especially on social media. (Families can have a brand, too.)

Communication and Relationships: in the workplace, our relational standards need to be even higher than in our personal lives. Communication, both written and oral, must be more formal and appropriate, and always tactful and courteous. In order to build a harmonious working environment, positivity and constructive communication are the order of the day. Also, many lifelong friendships are formed at work, where *mutuality* and *respect* guide our behavior (*especially* in mixed gender relationships).

Growth Mindset: successful people are committed to life-long learning. They grow their knowledge and skillsets through a wide variety of sources, and by observing the habits of interesting and resourceful people. Having an intrinsic mindset of continuous improvement is a hallmark of admired leaders.

As you can see, these are truly honorable qualities that show in our careers and throughout life. Professionalism is a huge self-confidence booster for your children, and is a telltale sign of excellent parental preparation. As mentioned earlier, *you will be more confident in letting go when your children demonstrate their ability to navigate the adult world.* It's as win-win as it gets.

TAKE FIVE

We encourage you to reflect on how well your children model the personal leadership skills described in this chapter. Which do they already possess and which are areas for further growth? Can you see how these powerful attributes are signs of wings in your children?

Remember, you're in the driver's seat in demonstrating and developing these skills. All of your efforts will pay off in a big way throughout their adult lives. Now that is something to be proud of!

CHAPTER EIGHT

DEALING WITH ANXIETY AND TECHNOLOGY

*"Worry never robs tomorrow of its sorrow,
it only saps today of its joy."*
—Leo Buscaglia

Recently, I (Dennis) had the pleasure of visiting with a principal from a small town in Wisconsin. During our wide-ranging conversation, he shared about the high levels of anxiety his high school students are exhibiting. You'd have to see their tranquil location to fully appreciate just how out of character this is. But, then again, research is abounding that today's students, whether in college or high school, are showing unprecedented levels of anxiety and depression.

We believe this condition is a natural consequence of how well children are being trained (or not), their often excessive exposure to social media and screens (versus real-life relationships and activities), and the high levels of pressure they are experiencing on a number of levels. We also believe it's largely up to us as parents, educators, youth leaders and mentors, and other caring adults to accept responsibility and reverse this course. The very futures and socio-emotional health of our kids are at stake. With that in mind, here are nine areas where we believe parents can play a powerful *preventive* role:

1. *Parenting style.* In our desire to see our children successful and happy, we sometimes employ parenting methods
that unwittingly heighten adolescent anxiety. Whether
from the intense pressures of a performance parent, the
overbearing micromanagement of a helicopter parent,
or the leniency of a permissive parent, well-meaning
parents can stunt their children's growth, maturation,
and self-confidence. This only serves to compound the
already-high stress levels common during the teen years.

2. *Family pace.* Sometimes our lives are so busy that it
seems we're on a treadmill set at warp speed. Parents, we
are putting (or permitting) our children on that treadmill, and it's depriving them of balance and the time
they need to enjoy nature, reflect, chill, pray, play, nap,
read a book, or just hang out without the overhang of
countless activities. For introverts and kids who operate
at a slower pace, this can be draining or worse. How is
your family's pace? Are you consciously building mar-
gin into your children's schedules to maintain balance
and keep their tanks full?

3. *Resumé building obsession/perfectionistic tendencies.* The
tagline for the Lexus luxury car company is the "relentless pursuit of perfection," and how well this describes
many teens today! Whether the pressure is coming from
parents or schools or is self-inflicted, teens are stressing
out over their assumed need for the perfect resumé to
succeed. An urgent priority is to disabuse them of this
notion. Nowadays, pressures previously felt in the adult
years are robbing many kids of a childhood. Whether
it's all AP courses, a GPA fixation, or participation

(better yet, leadership) in clubs or organizations, resumé building often dominates the high school years. What "success messages" are you sending to your children? Is their best good enough for you?

4. *Self-awareness and self-care.* Compared with yesteryear, today's teens face greater pressures and a more competitive world. For example, with "college for all" messaging and growing pressures to know what careers they should pursue or which college to attend, high schoolers are naturally anxious. At a time when students are still discovering WHO they are, this is placing the cart before the horse. Parents, you can do your children a great service by promoting *self-awareness* of their skills, talents, interests, personal nature, and passions. Also, be sure to help your children understand, prevent, and manage their stressors by fostering self-care and healthy living (e.g., diet, physical activity, and adequate rest). How well do your children know themselves and their stressors? These are vitally important, wings-building conversations to have with your kids.

5. *Social drama and unhealthy relationships.* Although the anxiety-laden social lives of teens probably date back to the Stone Age, the advent of social media takes it to an entirely new level. Much has been written on the subject, so we simply want to emphasize a few things. One is for your teen to be self-aware of the impact social media has on his/her life in terms of stressors, privacy, and relationships. Two is for them to be highly selective in making friends with positive and productive people who share their interests and values. Three is for them to

steer clear of social drama and gossip. Finally, if they're experiencing pain or anxiety from a breakup or no invitation/acceptance to the big school event, reassure them their identity and value in no way lies in a romantic relationship or in popularity with the opposite sex. That's a pressure you definitely want to nip in the bud!

6. *Tech vs. relational engagement.* With the addictive nature of smartphones and screens, teens, parents, and entire families are losing something besides their attention spans: relational intimacy and engagement. Initially, it affected teens most, but increasingly it has become an issue for parents as well. Parents, this is where tough love and good modeling will pay dividends. Value face-to-face time over tech time and be mindful of whether your teen's screens might be contributing to anxiety or loneliness.

7. *Family dysfunction and inadequate support systems.* From a child's standpoint, one of the greatest sources of emotional stability and security is being part of a loving, well-functioning family. However, one of the greatest societal changes over the last several decades has been the deterioration in this system. For example, today, just 69% of children are living in two-parent families, due in large part to births from unmarried parents and to divorce. While every situation is unique, and many, many healthy children are growing up in loving single-parent families, we must be sensitive to the impact our family situations are having on our children. This includes taking active steps to ensure they have other caring adult men and women involved in their lives.

8. *Insufficient preparation for independence.* As mentioned, we have a systemic problem in that parents and educators often assume the other is building the life skills students need to succeed. So, predictably, many important skills are falling through the cracks. In addition to practical skills like cooking, banking, and budgeting, personal leadership skills are often de-emphasized in favor of traditional subjects required by colleges. Parents, let's not assume our kids are learning it in school. Too often, they're not.

9. *Setting appropriate "anxiety boundaries."* Students who are heading to college will soon find themselves in an anxiety fishbowl. They will be surrounded by other students who are facing their own pressures and stressors, and it's easy to fall into the trap of shouldering their burdens as well as our own. Of course, we want to be empathetic and a good friend to others, but it's critical to maintain healthy boundaries, especially when we have our own significant pressures to bear. This is an important topic to raise with your children ahead of time.

There are several other ways parents can help prevent anxiety in children. For one, you can always keep your cool no matter how volatile the topic, and remember that *you were a teen once.* It's so easy to apply our current wisdom as adults to their age and stage! Second, be careful not to "over share" the various challenges and situations you are facing in your own life. The last thing they need is to take on your stress. Finally, always remember the importance of having fun together, and let them do the picking and choosing. You might just learn a thing or two!

Coping and Resilience Strategies

To state the obvious, even our best prevention strategies don't cover all of life's challenges. And, when hard stuff happens to our children, parents carry a special burden. (Nicole Helget certainly captured this when she said, "A mother is only as happy as her unhappiest child.") As much as we might wish that the path to fulfillment is a straight line, it's not. In our personal lives, adversity and anxiety can come from loss, disappointments, mistakes, underperformance, breakups, mistreatment, family struggles, financial stress, health challenges, and more. Teens and young adults experience additional stressors from grades, friendships, and college/career decisions. And, if they hang out with stressed-out friends, it can easily rub off.

We all respond so differently to adversity, don't we? Some of us are consumed by fear or worry, and tend to focus more on the problem and our current circumstances than on potential solutions and constructive steps. Others, after the initial shock or disappointment wears off, go into "problem-solving mode" and may actually even be energized by it. They reject the victim mentality and pity parties and instead show *perseverance, persistence, determination, grit, adaptability, and courage.* This is resilience, and it's an essential quality to build in our children.

Although adversity can be brutal and challenging, there is a silver lining. For example, it is the surest way to character and personal growth. Also, it provides valuable experience and wisdom to handle future situations. And, it equips us to inspire and encourage others who are facing similar challenges. That's huge.

So, how do we build resilience and help our children cope with the stressors they're already experiencing? Here are some perspectives to share with your children that we describe in detail in *What I Wish I Knew at 18:*

» Remember, adversity is part of all of our lives and can be preparation for *even greater* things

» Remind yourself of the classic saying that "day follows night." Try to see the other side of the valley, so to speak. Don't view today's low point as your "new normal."

» Release your pain and worries using constructive stress outlets, your support system, and by taking care of your health. By all means, don't go it alone.

» Take seemingly insurmountable challenges one step at a time. It reduces our fears and builds momentum.

» Always keep the faith and focus on the problem and what you can control.

» If you feel consumed by the problem, "project" it onto a third party and imagine giving advice to them. It's a great way to stay objective!

"A bend in the road is not the end of the road unless we fail to make the turn."
—Author Unknown

"You may not realize it when it happens, but a kick in the teeth may be the best thing in the world for you."
—Walt Disney

A Few Words On Technology

No modern parenting book would be complete without some commentary on technology. Notwithstanding the good that comes from it, the adverse side effects are real and pervasive: shorter attention spans, relational distance, heightened loneliness and reclusiveness, increased anxiety and agitation, addiction to being entertained, sleep deprivation, lack of motivation, and impaired communication and social skills. Can you imagine the labels if technology was regulated by the FDA?!?

To add insult to injury, technology has become the battleground among families everywhere. At LifeSmart, our conversations with parents often go like this:

> Parent: My son has no motivation. All he wants to do is play videogames. What should I do?
>
> Dennis/Arlyn: Didn't you just answer your own question?
>
> Parent: Yeah, you're probably right.

Now, let's contrast this issue with a family trip to the grocery store. For good reasons, we take active steps to minimize our time spent in the candy, soda, and snack aisles. Why? We want our kids to be healthy. But, interestingly, when it comes to screens and devices, we give them the entire store despite the adverse consequences we are seeing everywhere, *including in our own children*—consequences that *far exceed* an occasional chocolate or snack binge! In too many cases, parents are abdicating their responsibility and authority when it comes to the tech arena and it's showing. Why? It occupies our kids, and in the moment, keeps them happy. Simply put, there is too much at stake in our kids' health, relationships, and productivity if we don't take necessary steps to manage these risks. Yes, even if it takes tough love.

Many experts have written extensively on this subject so we will not belabor the point. But, we do want to lend our support with some common sense recommendations:

» Have frank, big-picture conversations of the benefits and risks of technology, including the research showing the adverse side effects when not handled with responsibility and maturity. Peer pressure regarding technology and social media is acute, so they'll appreciate the background perspective to understand where you're coming from. Like other sensitive subjects, your conversations should be open but real regarding the potential risks and consequences.

» It's your phone that you are leasing to them, not theirs. With a lease, there is a written contract whose terms must be adhered to in order to extend the privilege. Why should your child's phone be any different? There are sample contracts out there you can appropriate and adapt for your purposes . . . review the terms and mutually agree on the consequences. And, then, steadfastly enforce them if/when the terms are breached. Consistency is key—otherwise you'll lose their respect.

» Implement something along the lines of a "no phone in your room 30 minutes before bedtime" rule. And, it should be charged in a location inaccessible to your children. It is a well-researched fact that their sleep habits are at stake if you don't.

» Create screen time limits on weeknights and weekends, and declare the dining room table a "no-phone zone" during mealtime. Set a limit for how much screen time is allowed on school nights based on their responsibilities and observed side effects.

» Incorporate age- and responsibility-based parental controls on devices.

» Share articles and research on the wise use (and consequences of disabuse) of technology. Keep the lines of communication open with your teen so you are sharing with them *why* you are making the guidelines you are making. Adapt these as time goes on and demonstrated responsibility grows. Guidelines may also vary from child-to-child within your family, based on varying ages and maturity levels.

» Help them build their own self-awareness of the effects technology may be having on them and how to manage these risks.

» Ignore peer pressure from other parents whose family policies regarding technology are more lenient than yours.

Finally, technology is a fabulous topic for addressing time management and the concept of *opportunity cost*. With each passing year, your children's success will increasingly depend on how well they manage their time. So, when it comes to the recreational use of technology, a revealing question for your children is what they would be doing otherwise (i.e., the opportunity). Would they instead be playing outside, spending quality family time together, reading a book, working a part-time job, volunteering, learning a new skill, or otherwise? Too many young people aren't considering these important tradeoffs, and it's up to parents to raise the issue.

TAKE FIVE

1. How would you assess your child's anxiety level? How do they best cope with daily stressors? Which prevention and coping strategies discussed might help manage these risks?

2. How are you dealing with technology and screen time in your home? How is it affecting your children and are they aware of it? How are you setting and enforcing boundaries to reduce the common side effects of technology use?

3. Are your children spending their time on what's most important? What disciplines will they take with them after they leave home? The answers to these vital questions will influence how well they navigate their launch into the real world.

CONCLUSION

The ability to successfully launch teens to soar in adulthood is the result of all of the hard work and preparation that has come before. Their self-confidence as independent adults, and your willingness and ability to move out of the driver seat, will frame how well they transition to this next phase of life.

As we empower and confidently release our teens into the world, it helps to remember our own lives at that stage. We made many mistakes (didn't we?), but eventually we found our way. We learned how to do laundry, schedule our courses, change majors and careers, make new friends, manage our time and money, live on our own, and overcome adversity. Our parents didn't know about all of the micro decisions and mistakes we made—and truthfully, isn't that a good thing?!

The fact is, we can't control our children's outcomes, but we can prepare them to make wise decisions for their long-term futures. We need to let them find their way, while always being there for sharing, caring, and advice as they seek it. And, then we let go, knowing we've given it our best.

It's as simple and as difficult as that!

The View from the Back Seat

There will come a time when your conversations begin to change—in a great way. Just like the joy you experienced teaching them sports or how to ride a bike—you will now enjoy a new and mature relationship, as they make adult decisions and willingly listen to (and even solicit) your advice. They will say things that make you realize that more of your words sunk in during their teen years than you ever thought! (At this point, we encourage you to resist with all your might the temptation to say, "I told you so!")

You will talk about things you've never discussed before, and they will recognize your value in new ways. Whether it's how to cook a meal, how to know if the man or woman they've just met could be "the one," how to land that dream job, or how to deal with some adversity, they will come to appreciate your wisdom and perspective. Yes, they've finally outgrown the "teen pride" stage and entered the "mom and dad are smarter than we thought" stage. Hallelujah! And, you will smile each time, knowing the relationship you've built along the way is an enduring one. They still need you, but in a different way—just as it should be.

But, for now, please know that we applaud you for taking this time to invest in your parenting growth. As you reflect on this book, you'll no doubt find areas you already model well (kudos!), and some others where you could stand to improve. It's that way for each of us, including these authors! We're all works in progress, and, by adopting a growth mindset, you can take your parenting to a new level. Forget about perfection and simply strive to be the best you can be.

Having a healthy frame of mind is essential, too. That means taking proper care of yourself and tapping into your support system so you can share your triumphs and concerns with others. We often say that parenting is a team sport, and it's so true. And, by extending yourself grace and remaining hopeful, you can face and overcome the challenges and natural feelings of inadequacy every parent experiences.

After reading this book, we hope you feel encouraged and equipped with a solid philosophical framework and some concrete action steps to help you prepare your family for a successful launch. Please let us know how it's going. We're right there, cheering for you and your children.

To WINGS!

PARENTING CHECKLIST

Life Perspective

- » Do they understand their unique gifts, talents, passions, and worth?
- » Do they have a positive outlook on life?
- » Do they know how to live life strategically and with discipline and purpose?
- » Are they focused on others before themselves?
- » Are they committed to developing a wide range of interests?
- » Are they willing to take risks, even if they might not succeed?
- » Do they project a positive, can-do attitude?
- » Do they accept that life isn't necessarily fair?
- » Are they adaptable to changing circumstances?

Character:

- » Do they readily demonstrate love, compassion, and service to others?
- » Are they guided by integrity in their actions
- » and words?
- » Do they stand up for their beliefs and values with conviction?
- » Are they committed to giving everything their best effort?

» Do they take full responsibility for their mistakes and shortfalls?

» Do they demonstrate humility in their successes and recognize others?

» Are they open to receiving constructive feedback?

» Do they serve as an encourager, rather than a critic, to others?

» Do they act as a role model when around younger people?

Relationships and Communication:

» Do they prioritize relationships with others over possessions and power?

» Are they comfortable expressing their feelings and emotions to others?

» Do they build friendships with people who share their values, beliefs, and interests?

» Do they avoid destructive, negative people who don't have their interests at heart and understand that everyone is not meant to be their friend?

» Do they know how to make a great first impression and communicate effectively with adults?

» Do they demonstrate excellent listening skills and fully engage in conversation?

» Do they regularly show appreciation and gratitude toward others?

» Do they know how to disagree in an agreeable manner?

Adversity and Spirituality:

> » Are they prepared to accept that adversity happens, builds our character, and often makes sense after the fact?
> » Do they persevere through trials and disappointments?
> » Can they count their blessings and demonstrate a grateful heart even in trials?
> » Do they know how to release stress and pain in a healthy and patient manner?
> » Are they committed to learning from their mistakes?
> » Do they know how to cultivate the elements necessary for a thriving spiritual life?
> » Do they reserve time for daily reflection, prayer, or meditation?
> » Can they look at trials as an opportunity to build their faith?

Personal Productivity and Life Skills:

> » Are they an effective goal setter, planner, time manager, and decision maker?
> » Are they a responsible and self-disciplined user of technology?
> » Are they comfortable speaking in groups and leading discussions?
> » Are they discerning and skeptical of what they read and hear in the news media?
> » Do they have a disciplined study method that works in high pressure situations?

» Do they know how to change a tire, cook/eat healthy, do laundry, fill out applications, make appointments, grocery shop, demonstrate good manners, develop a compelling resumé, and conduct a job interview?

Career Selection and Advancement:

» Do they know how to comprehensively assess their interests, skills, lifestyle preferences, and training desires to select a well-matched career?

» Do they understand how to build a winning competitive edge and effectively market themselves to potential employers?

» Do they fully understand the qualities that employers value in their star employees?

» Do they understand the importance of networking and the job search process?

Love and Family:

» Do they understand the difference between "love" and "lust" and that love takes time and the right timing?

» Do they know that the keys to responsible dating involve being *discriminating, discerning, and deliberate?*

» Will they approach marriage as a truly forever decision?

» Are they committed to fully examining their compatibility before marrying?

» Do they know the key qualities of successful, long-term marriages?

» Do they understand that the three best ways to avoid poverty are to graduate from high school, not marry before 20, and only have children after they marry?

Financial Management:

» Do they understand the basics of being financially literate and how to be a wise steward, productive earner, savvy consumer, cautious debtor, disciplined saver, and cheerful giver?

» Do they know how to live within their means and manage a budget?

» Do they know how to prudently use credit and to pay off their balances monthly?

» Do they know the importance of investing early, regularly, and as much as possible in a disciplined and diversified long-term investment program?

» Do they understand the workings of the economy and financial markets?

» Do they know how to invest and manage their bank accounts?

» Do they know the importance of giving first, investing second, and spending last?

» Do they know how to build a solid credit rating?

» Do they know the ways to avoid identity theft?

Parenting Style and Upcoming Transition:

» Are you adapting your parenting style from "control" to "influence"?

» Do they know how much you love them, value them, and *believe* in them?

» Are you actively finding ways to seek out their opinions and help with decisions?

» Do you regularly share time together at the time and place of their choosing?

» Are you prepared to let them go and be their "encouragers in chief?"

» Have you shared the key transition risks with them: social impatience, lack of study disciplines, damaging recreational habits, lack of a support network, excessive performance stress, and financial irresponsibility?

ENDNOTES

1. Sasse, Ben, *The Vanishing American Adult,* St. Martins Press, New York, New York: 2017.

2. *The Condition of Education* 2017, (NCES 2017-144), U.S. Department of Education.

3. Itzkowitz, Michael, "New Data Further Cements Completion Crisis in Higher Education," *Third Way,* February 1, 2018.

4. "Retention and Graduation Rates," *College Transitions and U.S. Department of Education* (2015).

5. "On Second Thought: U.S. Adults Reflect on Their Education Decisions," *Gallup-Strada Educational Network;* and Busteed, Brandon, "Do You Regret Your College Choices?" *Gallup Blog,* June 1, 2017.

6. 2015 Annual Report, *Penn State Center for Collegiate Mental Health.*

MEET THE AUTHORS

We are Dennis Trittin and Arlyn Lawrence, co-authors and speakers at LifeSmart Publishing. Our mission is to empower and equip the next generation with the leadership and life skills to succeed in adulthood. Through books, curriculum, our blog, and speaking engagements, we bring practical resources to teens and the adults and organizations guiding them. As authors, parents, and mentors, we share a passion for young people and have a special affinity for parents navigating the challenging teen years.

Our seminal work, *What I Wish I Knew at 18,* trains young people to flourish by revealing the practices of honorable and successful leaders. This book and curriculum are now serving families, schools, and youth mentoring organizations around the world. These resources have proven especially valuable for parents as a third-party voice of wisdom for their children.

Subsequently, we co-authored *Parenting for the Launch: Raising Teens to Succeed in the Real World* to prepare parents and families for the launch. This book helps parents cover the bases, build a strong and enduring relationship with their teen, and position for this important milestone. Written by a father and mother from two different families that have launched seven children between them, we bring a variety of parenting perspectives to our global audience.

Our past roles—Dennis in business leadership and Arlyn in child and family development—give us valuable lenses to view life preparedness. Our current roles put us squarely in the thought arena of what is happening with teens and emerging adults. Because we're involved in the business, educator, and mentoring sectors, we regularly hear feedback about the training deficit in today's adolescents. And, a members of parent communities ourselves, we are keenly aware of the emotions and concerns surrounding the launch of children into the real world.

Each of us was raised by loving parents and have strong, grown families of our own. We know the influence and impact that healthy, intentional parenting can have on children. At the same time, we see the huge need for more parents to be equipped and encouraged in their vital role. This is especially true as kids approach the middle to late teen years and their transition into adulthood is within view.

Don't be surprised if you feel a little convicted by this book . . . we invariably experience it ourselves as we write and share on these topics, with the benefit of 20-20 hindsight! We are the first to admit we are not perfect parents, nor do we have perfect children. But the goal is not to be perfect parents, just better parents doing the best we can.

It's our joy and privilege to serve other parents who desire to set their children up for every success in life and to build a strong relationship that will endure in the adult years. Thank you for inviting us into your family and your parenting, and best wishes for a successful launch.

Dennis Trittin

Prior to his most recent career as an author, publisher, educator, mentor, and speaker, Dennis was a successful investment manager and senior executive for 28 years with Russell Investments. During his career, Dennis researched and evaluated thousands of investment leaders worldwide, giving him a unique perspective to share the strategies and practices of successful people.

As founder and President of LifeSmart Publishing, Dennis now devotes his life to equipping young people to succeed. His books, *What I Wish I Knew at 18: Life Lessons for the Road Ahead* and *Parenting for the Launch: Raising Teens to Succeed in the Real World,* are fulfilling this mission on a global basis. Through resources, speaking engagements, and his blog, Dennis serves young people and the parents, educators, and mentors guiding them.

Also, he has served as board chair and life skills teacher at Lighthouse Christian School and a deacon at his church. Dennis holds a Bachelor of Business Administration degree from the University of Wisconsin and a Master of Business Administration degree from the University of Washington, where he was Valedictorian. He also is a

Chartered Financial Analyst. On the home front, Dennis has been married to his wife, Jeanne, for 36 years. They have two grown children and make their home in Gig Harbor, Washington.

Arlyn Lawrence

Arlyn Lawrence is the editor, curriculum developer, co-author, and seminar leader for LifeSmart Publishing, including the *What I Wish I Knew at 18* book and leadership course, and *Parenting for the Launch: Raising Teens to Succeed in the Real World*. She is the founder and president of Inspira Literary Solutions, an independent book publishing company; her background in publishing also includes freelance writing and editing, curriculum development, and magazine editing/publishing, as well as her current work as a book editor and publishing project manager. A published author and international seminar leader emphasizing children and family leadership, she equips parents and educators with vision, perspective, and practical solutions. She is a graduate of the University of Maryland.

Arlyn spent fourteen years homeschooling her five children before they entered the public school system, and over fifteen years as an educational director for youth and children's programming. She is actively involved in youth/young adult mentoring and also enjoys speaking to and interacting with parents, educators, and youth mentors. She and her husband, Doug, have been married for 36 years and, in addition to their five grown children, are delighted to have six grandchildren. They reside in Fox Island, Washington.

WE'D LOVE TO HEAR FROM YOU!

———————— ⌄ ————————

We hope you enjoyed our book!
Please keep in touch.
You can find us:

On our websites:
www.parentingforthelaunch.com,
www.dennistrittin.com

By email:
dtrittin@dennistrittin.com,
arlyn@lifesmartpublishing.com

By signing up for our email newsletter:
http://www.dennistrittin.com/newsletter.aspx

On Facebook:
www.facebook.com/parentingforthelaunch
www.facebook.com/dennistrittinfan
("Like" us!)

On Twitter:
www.twitter.com/parent4launch
www.twitter.com/arlynlawrence
("Follow" us!)

———————— ⌃ ————————

Also Available
from LifeSmart Publishing:

Parenting for the Launch is a complete parenting guide for raising today's teens to flourish in adulthood. It inspires and equips parents with innovative strategies to build essential leadership skills, develop a strong and enduring relationship, and position for a successful launch after graduation.

Few transitions bring as much joy, tears, and anxiety to parents as when their children leave home and begin life on their own. Endorsed by parenting experts, educators, employers, and mentors alike, *Parenting for the Launch* will help you parent with purpose and let go with confidence!

ISBN 978-0-9832526-7-2

Available at www.dennistrittin.com and

www.amazon.com

Also Available from LifeSmart Publishing:

What I Wish I Knew at 18 is an engaging, comprehensive, and conversational book written to help young adults achieve success in life, providing:

- 109 success pointers for a soaring launch into adulthood
- practical, road-tested wisdom in key life arenas as life perspective, character, relationships and communication, spiritual life, handling adversity, personal productivity, college academics, career selection and advancement, love and marriage, and managing finances

Unique in scope, universal in its message, and timely in its wisdom, *What I Wish I Knew at 18* serves as an invaluable life coach for young people and destination guide for parents. Together with *Parenting for the Launch*, it offers parents and guardians an essential "third party voice" that strengthens relationships and shares practical wisdom for life.

ISBN 978-0-9832526-0-3

Available at www.dennistrittin.com

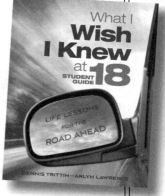